Mastering Apache Storm

Processing big data streams in real time

Ankit Jain

BIRMINGHAM - MUMBAI

Mastering Apache Storm

First published: August 2017

Production reference: 1140817

Published by Packt Publishing Ltd.
Livery Place
35 Livery Street
Birmingham
B3 2PB, UK.
ISBN 978-1-78712-563-6

www.packtpub.com

Credits

Author
Ankit Jain

Reviewers
Doug Ortiz
Oleg Okun

Commissioning Editor
Veena Pagare

Acquisition Editor
Divya Poojari

Content Development Editor
Mayur Pawanikar

Technical Editor
Dinesh Pawar

Copy Editor
Safis Editing

Project Coordinator
Nidhi Joshi

Proofreader
Safis Editing

Indexer
Tejal Daruwale Soni

Graphics
Tania Dutta

Production Coordinator
Arvindkumar Gupta

About the Author

Ankit Jain holds a bachelor's degree in computer science and engineering. He has 6 years, experience in designing and architecting solutions for the big data domain and has been involved with several complex engagements. His technical strengths include Hadoop, Storm, S4, HBase, Hive, Sqoop, Flume, Elasticsearch, machine learning, Kafka, Spring, Java, and J2EE.

He also shares his thoughts on his personal blog. You can follow him on Twitter at `@mynameisanky`. He spends most of his time reading books and playing with different technologies. When not at work, he spends time with his family and friends watching movies and playing games.

About the Reviewers

Doug Ortiz is a senior big data artechitect at ByteCubed who has been architecting, developing and integrating enterprise solutions throughout his whole career. Organizations that leverage high skillset have been able to rediscover and reuse their underutilized data via existing and emerging technologies such as: Microsoft BI Stack, Hadoop, NoSQL Databases, SharePoint, Hadoop, related toolsets and technologies.

He is the founder of Illustris, LLC and can be reached at dougortiz@illustris.org.

Interesting aspects of his profession:

- He has experience integrating multiple platforms and products
- He has big data, data science certifications, R and Python certifications
- He helps organizations gain a deeper understanding of, and value, their current investments in data and existing resources, turning them into useful sources of information
- He has improved, salvaged, and architected projects by utilizing unique and innovative techniques

His hobbies are yoga and scuba diving.

Oleg Okun is a machine learning expert and the author/editor of four books, numerous journal articles, and conference papers. His career spans more than a quarter of a century. He was employed in both academia and industry in his mother country, Belarus, and abroad (Finland, Sweden, and Germany). His work experience includes document image analysis, fingerprint biometrics, bioinformatics, online/offline marketing analytics, credit scoring analytics, and text analytics.

He is interested in all aspects of distributed machine learning and the Internet of Things. Oleg currently lives and works in Hamburg, Germany.

I would like to express my deepest gratitude to my parents for everything that they have done for me.

www.PacktPub.com

For support files and downloads related to your book, please visit www.PacktPub.com. Did you know that Packt offers eBook versions of every book published, with PDF and ePub files available? You can upgrade to the eBook version at www.PacktPub.com, and as a print book customer, you are entitled to a discount on the eBook copy.

Get in touch with us at service@packtpub.com for more details. At www.PacktPub.com, you can also read a collection of free technical articles, sign up for a range of free newsletters and receive exclusive discounts and offers on Packt books and eBooks.

https://www.packtpub.com/mapt

Get the most in-demand software skills with Mapt. Mapt gives you full access to all Packt books and video courses, as well as industry-leading tools to help you plan your personal development and advance your career.

Why subscribe?

- Fully searchable across every book published by Packt
- Copy and paste, print, and bookmark content
- On demand and accessible via a web browser

Customer Feedback

Thanks for purchasing this Packt book. At Packt, quality is at the heart of our editorial process. To help us improve, please leave us an honest review on this book's Amazon page at https://www.amazon.com/dp/1787125637.

If you'd like to join our team of regular reviewers, you can e-mail us at customerreviews@packtpub.com. We award our regular reviewers with free eBooks and videos in exchange for their valuable feedback. Help us be relentless in improving our products.

Table of Contents

Preface

Real-time data processing in no longer a luxury exercised by a few big companies but has become a necessity for businesses that want to compete, and Apache Storm is one of the de facto standards for developing real-time processing pipelines. The key features of Storm are that it is horizontally scalable, is fault tolerant, and provides guaranteed message processing. Storm can solve various types of analytic problem: machine learning, log processing, graph analysis, and so on.

Mastering Storm will serve both as a *getting started* guide to inexperienced developers and as a reference for implementing advanced use cases with Storm for experienced developers. In the first two chapters, you will learn the basics of a Storm topology and various components of a Storm cluster. In the later chapters, you will learn how to build a Storm application that can interact with various other big data technologies and how to create transactional topologies. Finally, the last two chapters cover case studies for log processing and machine learning. We are also going to cover how we can use the Storm scheduler to assign delicate work to delicate machines.

What this book covers

Chapter 1, *Real-Time Processing and Storm Introduction*, gives an introduction to Storm and its components.

Chapter 2, *Storm Deployment, Topology Development, and Topology* Options, covers deploying Storm into the cluster, deploying the sample topology on a Storm cluster, how we can monitor the storm pipeline using storm UI, and how we can dynamically change the log level settings.

Chapter 3, *Storm Parallelism and Data Partitioning*, covers the parallelism of topology, how to configure parallelism at the code level, guaranteed message processing, and Storm internally generated tuples.

Chapter 4, *Trident Introduction*, covers an introduction to Trident, an understanding of the Trident data model, and how we can write Trident filters and functions. This chapter also covers repartitioning and aggregation operations on Trident tuples.

Chapter 5, *Trident Topology and Uses*, introduces Trident tuple grouping, non-transactional topology, and a sample Trident topology. The chapter also introduces Trident state and distributed RPC.

Chapter 6, *Storm Scheduler*, covers different types of scheduler available in Storm: the default scheduler, isolation scheduler, resource-aware scheduler, and custom scheduler.

Chapter 7, *Monitoring of the Storm Cluster*, covers monitoring Storm by writing custom monitoring UIs using the stats published by Nimbus. We explain the integration of Ganglia with Storm using JMXTrans. This chapter also covers how we can configure Storm to publish JMX metrics.

Chapter 8, *Integration of Storm and Kafka*, shows the integration of Storm with Kafka. This chapter starts with an introduction to Kafka, covers the installation of Storm, and ends with the integration of Storm with Kafka to solve any real-world problem.

Chapter 9, *Storm and Hadoop Integration*, covers an overview of Hadoop, writing the Storm topology to publish data into HDFS, an overview of Storm-YARN, and deploying the Storm topology on YARN.

Chapter 10, *Storm Integration with Redis, Elasticsearch, and HBase*, teaches you how to integrate Storm with various other big data technologies.

Chapter 11, *Apache Log Processing with Storm*, covers a sample log processing application in which we parse Apache web server logs and generate some business information from log files.

Chapter 12, *Twitter Tweets Collection and Machine Learning*, walks you through a case study implementing a machine learning topology in Storm.

What you need for this book

All of the code in this book has been tested on CentOS 6.5. It will run on other variants of Linux and Windows as well with appropriate changes in commands.

We have tried to keep the chapters self-contained, and the setup and installation of all the software used in each chapter are included in the chapter itself. These are the software packages used throughout the book:

- CentOS 6.5
- Oracle JDK 8
- Apache ZooKeeper 3.4.6
- Apache Storm 1.0.2
- Eclipse or Spring Tool Suite
- Elasticsearch 2.4.4
- Hadoop 2.2.2
- Logstash 5.4.1
- Kafka 0.9.0.1
- Esper 5.3.0

Who this book is for

If you are a Java developer and are keen to enter into the world of real-time stream processing applications using Apache Storm, then this book is for you. No previous experience in Storm is required as this book starts from the basics. After finishing this book, you will be able to develop not-so-complex Storm applications.

Conventions

In this book, you will find a number of text styles that distinguish between different kinds of information. Here are some examples of these styles and an explanation of their meaning. Code words in text, database table names, folder names, filenames, file extensions, pathnames, dummy URLs, user input, and Twitter handles are shown as follows: "Add the following line in the `storm.yaml` file of the Nimbus machine to enable JMX on the Nimbus node."

A block of code is set as follows:

```
<dependency>
  <groupId>org.apache.storm</groupId>
  <artifactId>storm-core</artifactId>
  <version>1.0.2</version>
  <scope>provided<scope>
</dependency>
```

Any command-line input or output is written as follows:

```
cd $ZK_HOME/conf
touch zoo.cfg
```

New terms and **important words** are shown in bold. Words that you see on the screen, for example, in menus or dialog boxes, appear in the text like this: "Now, click on the **Connect** button to view the metrics of the supervisor node."

 Warnings or important notes appear like this.

 Tips and tricks appear like this.

Reader feedback

Feedback from our readers is always welcome. Let us know what you think about this book-what you liked or disliked. Reader feedback is important for us as it helps us develop titles that you will really get the most out of. To send us general feedback, simply e-mail feedback@packtpub.com, and mention the book's title in the subject of your message. If there is a topic that you have expertise in and you are interested in either writing or contributing to a book, see our author guide at www.packtpub.com/authors.

Customer support

Now that you are the proud owner of a Packt book, we have a number of things to help you to get the most from your purchase.

Downloading the example code

You can download the example code files for this book from your account at `http://www.packtpub.com`. If you purchased this book elsewhere, you can visit `http://www.packtpub.com/support`, and register to have the files e-mailed directly to you. You can download the code files by following these steps:

1. Log in or register to our website using your e-mail address and password.
2. Hover the mouse pointer on the **SUPPORT** tab at the top.
3. Click on **Code Downloads & Errata**.
4. Enter the name of the book in the **Search** box.
5. Select the book for which you're looking to download the code files.
6. Choose from the drop-down menu where you purchased this book from.
7. Click on **Code Download**.

Once the file is downloaded, please make sure that you unzip or extract the folder using the latest version of:

- WinRAR / 7-Zip for Windows
- Zipeg / iZip / UnRarX for Mac
- 7-Zip / PeaZip for Linux

The code bundle for the book is also hosted on GitHub at `https://github.com/PacktPublishing/Mastering-Apache-Storm`. We also have other code bundles from our rich catalog of books and videos available at `https://github.com/PacktPublishing/`. Check them out!

Downloading the color images of this book

We also provide you with a PDF file that has color images of the screenshots/diagrams used in this book. The color images will help you better understand the changes in the output. You can download this file from `https://www.packtpub.com/sites/default/files/downloads/MasteringApacheStorm_ColorImages.pdf`.

Errata

Although we have taken every care to ensure the accuracy of our content, mistakes do happen. If you find a mistake in one of our books-maybe a mistake in the text or the code-we would be grateful if you could report this to us. By doing so, you can save other readers from frustration and help us improve subsequent versions of this book. If you find any errata, please report them by visiting `http://www.packtpub.com/submit-errata`, selecting your book, clicking on the **Errata Submission Form** link, and entering the details of your errata. Once your errata are verified, your submission will be accepted and the errata will be uploaded to our website or added to any list of existing errata under the Errata section of that title. To view the previously submitted errata, go to `https://www.packtpub.com/books/content/support`, and enter the name of the book in the search field. The required information will appear under the **Errata** section.

Piracy

Piracy of copyrighted material on the Internet is an ongoing problem across all media. At Packt, we take the protection of our copyright and licenses very seriously. If you come across any illegal copies of our works in any form on the Internet, please provide us with the location address or website name immediately so that we can pursue a remedy. Please contact us at `copyright@packtpub.com` with a link to the suspected pirated material. We appreciate your help in protecting our authors and our ability to bring you valuable content.

Questions

If you have a problem with any aspect of this book, you can contact us at `questions@packtpub.com`, and we will do our best to address the problem.

1
Real-Time Processing and Storm Introduction

With the exponential growth in the amount of data being generated and advanced data-capturing capabilities, enterprises are facing the challenge of making sense out of this mountain of raw data. On the batch processing front, Hadoop has emerged as the go-to framework to deal with big data. Until recently, there has been a void when one looks for frameworks to build real-time stream processing applications. Such applications have become an integral part of a lot of businesses as they enable them to respond swiftly to events and adapt to changing situations. Examples of this are monitoring social media to analyze public response to any new product that you launch and predicting the outcome of an election based on the sentiments of election-related posts.

Organizations are collecting a large volume of data from external sources and want to evaluate/process the data in real time to get market trends, detect fraud, identify user behavior, and so on. The need for real-time processing is increasing day by day and we require a real-time system/platform that should support the following features:

- **Scalable**: The platform should be horizontally scalable without any down time.
- **Fault tolerance**: The platform should be able to process the data even after some of the nodes in a cluster go down.
- **No data lost**: The platform should provide the guaranteed processing of messages.
- **High throughput**: The system should be able to support millions of records per second and also support any size of messages.

- **Easy to operate**: The system should have easy installation and operation. Also, the expansion of clusters should be an easy process.
- **Multiple languages**: The platform should support multiple languages. The end user should be able to write code in different languages. For example, a user can write code in Python, Scala, Java, and so on. Also, we can execute different language code inside the one cluster.
- **Cluster isolation**: The system should support isolation so that dedicated processes can be assigned to dedicated machines for processing.

Apache Storm

Apache Storm has emerged as the platform of choice for industry leaders to develop distributed, real-time, data processing platforms. It provides a set of primitives that can be used to develop applications that can process a very large amount of data in real time in a highly scalable manner.

Storm is to real-time processing what Hadoop is to batch processing. It is open source software, and managed by Apache Software Foundation. It has been deployed to meet real-time processing needs by companies such as Twitter, Yahoo!, and Flipboard. Storm was first developed by Nathan Marz at BackType, a company that provided social search applications. Later, BackType was acquired by Twitter, and it is a critical part of their infrastructure. Storm can be used for the following use cases:

- **Stream processing**: Storm is used to process a stream of data and update a variety of databases in real time. This processing occurs in real time and the processing speed needs to match the input data speed.
- **Continuous computation**: Storm can do continuous computation on data streams and stream the results to clients in real time. This might require processing each message as it comes in or creating small batches over a short time. An example of continuous computation is streaming trending topics on Twitter into browsers.
- **Distributed RPC**: Storm can parallelize an intense query so that you can compute it in real time.
- **Real-time analytics**: Storm can analyze and respond to data that comes from different data sources as they happen in real time.

In this chapter, we will cover the following topics:

- What is a Storm?
- Features of Storm
- Architecture and components of a Storm cluster
- Terminologies of Storm
- Programming language
- Operation modes

Features of Storm

The following are some of the features of Storm that make it a perfect solution to process streams of data in real time:

- **Fast**: Storm has been reported to process up to 1 million tuples/records per second per node.
- **Horizontally scalable**: Being fast is a necessary feature to build a high volume/velocity data processing platform, but a single node will have an upper limit on the number of events that it can process per second. A node represents a single machine in your setup that executes Storm applications. Storm, being a distributed platform, allows you to add more nodes to your Storm cluster and increase the processing capacity of your application. Also, it is linearly scalable, which means that you can double the processing capacity by doubling the nodes.
- **Fault tolerant**: Units of work are executed by worker processes in a Storm cluster. When a worker dies, Storm will restart that worker, and if the node on which the worker is running dies, Storm will restart that worker on some other node in the cluster. This feature will be covered in more detail in `Chapter 3`, *Storm Parallelism and Data Partitioning*.
- **Guaranteed data processing**: Storm provides strong guarantees that each message entering a Storm process will be processed at least once. In the event of failures, Storm will replay the lost tuples/records. Also, it can be configured so that each message will be processed only once.
- **Easy to operate**: Storm is simple to deploy and manage. Once the cluster is deployed, it requires little maintenance.
- **Programming language agnostic**: Even though the Storm platform runs on **Java virtual machine** (**JVM**), the applications that run over it can be written in any programming language that can read and write to standard input and output streams.

Storm components

A Storm cluster follows a master-slave model where the master and slave processes are coordinated through ZooKeeper. The following are the components of a Storm cluster.

Nimbus

The Nimbus node is the master in a Storm cluster. It is responsible for distributing the application code across various worker nodes, assigning tasks to different machines, monitoring tasks for any failures, and restarting them as and when required.

Nimbus is stateless and stores all of its data in ZooKeeper. There is a single Nimbus node in a Storm cluster. If the active node goes down, then the passive node will become an Active node. It is designed to be fail-fast, so when the active Nimbus dies, the passive node will become an active node, or the down node can be restarted without having any effect on the tasks already running on the worker nodes. This is unlike Hadoop, where if the JobTracker dies, all the running jobs are left in an inconsistent state and need to be executed again. The Storm workers can work smoothly even if all the Nimbus nodes go down but the user can't submit any new jobs into the cluster or the cluster will not be able to reassign the failed workers to another node.

Supervisor nodes

Supervisor nodes are the worker nodes in a Storm cluster. Each supervisor node runs a supervisor daemon that is responsible for creating, starting, and stopping worker processes to execute the tasks assigned to that node. Like Nimbus, a supervisor daemon is also fail-fast and stores all of its states in ZooKeeper so that it can be restarted without any state loss. A single supervisor daemon normally handles multiple worker processes running on that machine.

The ZooKeeper cluster

In any distributed application, various processes need to coordinate with each other and share some configuration information. ZooKeeper is an application that provides all these services in a reliable manner. As a distributed application, Storm also uses a ZooKeeper cluster to coordinate various processes. All of the states associated with the cluster and the various tasks submitted to Storm are stored in ZooKeeper. Nimbus and supervisor nodes do not communicate directly with each other, but through ZooKeeper. As all data is stored in ZooKeeper, both Nimbus and the supervisor daemons can be killed abruptly without adversely affecting the cluster.

The following is an architecture diagram of a Storm cluster:

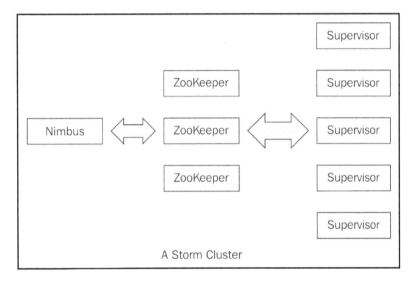

The Storm data model

The basic unit of data that can be processed by a Storm application is called a tuple. Each tuple consists of a predefined list of fields. The value of each field can be a byte, char, integer, long, float, double, Boolean, or byte array. Storm also provides an API to define your own datatypes, which can be serialized as fields in a tuple.

A tuple is dynamically typed, that is, you just need to define the names of the fields in a tuple and not their datatype. The choice of dynamic typing helps to simplify the API and makes it easy to use. Also, since a processing unit in Storm can process multiple types of tuples, it's not practical to declare field types.

Each of the fields in a tuple can be accessed by its name, `getValueByField(String)`, or its positional index, `getValue(int)`, in the tuple. Tuples also provide convenient methods such as `getIntegerByField(String)` that save you from typecasting the objects. For example, if you have a *Fraction (numerator, denominator)* tuple, representing fractional numbers, then you can get the value of the numerator by either using `getIntegerByField("numerator")` or `getInteger(0)`.

You can see the full set of operations supported by `org.apache.storm.tuple.Tuple` in the Java doc that is located at `https://storm.apache.org/releases/1.0.2/javadocs/org/apache/storm/tuple/Tuple.html`.

Definition of a Storm topology

In Storm terminology, a topology is an abstraction that defines the graph of the computation. You create a Storm topology and deploy it on a Storm cluster to process data. A topology can be represented by a direct acyclic graph, where each node does some kind of processing and forwards it to the next node(s) in the flow. The following diagram is a sample Storm topology:

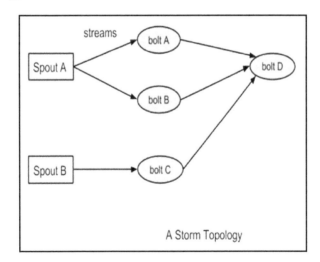

The following are the components of a Storm topology:

- **Tuple**: A single message/record that flows between the different instances of a topology is called a tuple.
- **Stream**: The key abstraction in Storm is that of a stream. A stream is an unbounded sequence of tuples that can be processed in parallel by Storm. Each stream can be processed by a single or multiple types of bolts (the processing units in Storm, which are defined later in this section). Thus, Storm can also be viewed as a platform to transform streams. In the preceding diagram, streams are represented by arrows. Each stream in a Storm application is given an ID and the bolts can produce and consume tuples from these streams on the basis of their ID. Each stream also has an associated schema for the tuples that will flow through it.
- **Spout**: A spout is the source of tuples in a Storm topology. It is responsible for reading or listening to data from an external source, for example, by reading from a log file or listening for new messages in a queue and publishing them--emitting in Storm terminology into streams. A spout can emit multiple streams, each of a different schema. For example, it can read records of 10 fields from a log file and emit them as different streams of seven-fields tuples and four-fields tuples each.

  The `org.apache.storm.spout.ISpout` interface is the interface used to define spouts. If you are writing your topology in Java, then you should use `org.apache.storm.topology.IRichSpout` as it declares methods to use with the `TopologyBuilder` API. Whenever a spout emits a tuple, Storm tracks all the tuples generated while processing this tuple, and when the execution of all the tuples in the graph of this source tuple is complete, it will send an acknowledgement back to the spout. This tracking happens only if a message ID was provided when emitting the tuple. If null was used as the message ID, this tracking will not happen.

  A tuple processing timeout can also be defined for a topology, and if a tuple is not processed within the specified timeout, a fail message will be sent back to the spout. Again, this will happen only if you define a message ID. A small performance gain can be extracted out of Storm at the risk of some data loss by disabling the message acknowledgements, which can be done by skipping the message ID while emitting tuples.

The important methods of spout are:

- `nextTuple()`: This method is called by Storm to get the next tuple from the input source. Inside this method, you will have the logic of reading data from external sources and emitting them to an instance of `org.apache.storm.spout.ISpoutOutputCollector`. The schema for streams can be declared by using the `declareStream` method of `org.apache.storm.topology.OutputFieldsDeclarer`.

  If a spout wants to emit data to more than one stream, it can declare multiple streams using the `declareStream` method and specify a stream ID while emitting the tuple. If there are no more tuples to emit at the moment, this method will not be blocked. Also, if this method does not emit a tuple, then Storm will wait for 1 millisecond before calling it again. This waiting time can be configured using the `topology.sleep.spout.wait.strategy.time.ms` setting.

- `ack(Object msgId)`: This method is invoked by Storm when the tuple with the given message ID is completely processed by the topology. At this point, the user should mark the message as processed and do the required cleaning up, such as removing the message from the message queue so that it does not get processed again.

- `fail(Object msgId)`: This method is invoked by Storm when it identifies that the tuple with the given message ID has not been processed successfully or has timed out of the configured interval. In such scenarios, the user should do the required processing so that the messages can be emitted again by the `nextTuple` method. A common way to do this is to put the message back in the incoming message queue.

- `open()`: This method is called only once--when the spout is initialized. If it is required to connect to an external source for the input data, define the logic to connect to the external source in the open method, and then keep fetching the data from this external source in the `nextTuple` method to emit it further.

Another point to note while writing your spout is that none of the methods should be blocking, as Storm calls all the methods in the same thread. Every spout has an internal buffer to keep track of the status of the tuples emitted so far. The spout will keep the tuples in this buffer until they are either acknowledged or failed, calling the `ack` or `fail` method, respectively. Storm will call the `nextTuple` method only when this buffer is not full.

- **Bolt**: A bolt is the processing powerhouse of a Storm topology and is responsible for transforming a stream. Ideally, each bolt in the topology should be doing a simple transformation of the tuples, and many such bolts can coordinate with each other to exhibit a complex transformation.

    The `org.apache.storm.task.IBolt` interface is preferably used to define bolts, and if a topology is written in Java, you should use the `org.apache.storm.topology.IRichBolt` interface. A bolt can subscribe to multiple streams of other components--either spouts or other bolts--in the topology and similarly can emit output to multiple streams. Output streams can be declared using the `declareStream` method of `org.apache.storm.topology.OutputFieldsDeclarer`.

    The important methods of a bolt are:

    - `execute(Tuple input)`: This method is executed for each tuple that comes through the subscribed input streams. In this method, you can do whatever processing is required for the tuple and then produce the output either in the form of emitting more tuples to the declared output streams, or other things such as persisting the results in a database.

        You are not required to process the tuple as soon as this method is called, and the tuples can be held until required. For example, while joining two streams, when a tuple arrives you can hold it until its counterpart also comes, and then you can emit the joined tuple.

The metadata associated with the tuple can be retrieved by the various methods defined in the `Tuple` interface. If a message ID is associated with a tuple, the execute method must publish an `ack` or `fail` event using `OutputCollector` for the bolt, or else Storm will not know whether the tuple was processed successfully. The `org.apache.storm.topology.IBasicBolt` interface is a convenient interface that sends an acknowledgement automatically after the completion of the execute method. If a fail event is to be sent, this method should throw `org.apache.storm.topology.FailedException`.

- `prepare(Map stormConf, TopologyContext context, OutputCollector collector)`: A bolt can be executed by multiple workers in a Storm topology. The instance of a bolt is created on the client machine and then serialized and submitted to Nimbus. When Nimbus creates the worker instances for the topology, it sends this serialized bolt to the workers. The work will desterilize the bolt and call the `prepare` method. In this method, you should make sure the bolt is properly configured to execute tuples. Any state that you want to maintain can be stored as instance variables for the bolt that can be serialized/deserialized later.

Operation modes in Storm

Operation modes indicate how the topology is deployed in Storm. Storm supports two types of operation modes to execute the Storm topology:

- **Local mode**: In local mode, Storm topologies run on the local machine in a single JVM. This mode simulates a Storm cluster in a single JVM and is used for the testing and debugging of a topology.
- **Remote mode**: In remote mode, we will use the Storm client to submit the topology to the master along with all the necessary code required to execute the topology. Nimbus will then take care of distributing your code.

In the next chapter, we are going to cover both local and remote mode in more detail, along with a sample example.

Programming languages

Storm was designed from the ground up to be usable with any programming language. At the core of Storm is a thrift definition for defining and submitting topologies. Since thrift can be used in any language, topologies can be defined and submitted in any language.

Similarly, spouts and bolts can be defined in any language. Non-JVM spouts and bolts communicate with Storm over a JSON-based protocol over `stdin`/`stdout`. Adapters that implement this protocol exist for Ruby, Python, JavaScript, and Perl. You can refer to `https://github.com/apache/storm/tree/master/storm-multilang` to find out about the implementation of these adapters.

Storm-starter has an example topology, `https://github.com/apache/storm/tree/master/examples/storm-starter/multilang/resources`, which implements one of the bolts in Python.

Summary

In this chapter, we introduced you to the basics of Storm and the various components that make up a Storm cluster. We saw a definition of different deployment/operation modes in which a Storm cluster can operate.

In the next chapter, we will set up a single and three-node Storm cluster and see how we can deploy the topology on a Storm cluster. We will also see different types of stream groupings supported by Storm and the guaranteed message semantic provided by Storm.

2
Storm Deployment, Topology Development, and Topology Options

In this chapter, we are going to start with deployment of Storm on multiple node (three Storm and three ZooKeeper) clusters. This chapter is very important because it focuses on how we can set up the production Storm cluster and why we need the high availability of both the Storm Supervisor, Nimbus, and ZooKeeper (as Storm uses ZooKeeper for storing the metadata of the cluster, topology, and so on)?

The following are the key points that we are going to cover in this chapter:

- Deployment of the Storm cluster
- Program and deploy the word count example
- Different options of the Storm UI--kill, active, inactive, and rebalance
- Walkthrough of the Storm UI
- Dynamic log level settings
- Validating the Nimbus high availability

Storm prerequisites

You should have the Java JDK and ZooKeeper ensemble installed before starting the deployment of the Storm cluster.

Installing Java SDK 7

Perform the following steps to install the Java SDK 7 on your machine. You can also go with JDK 1.8:

1. Download the Java SDK 7 RPM from Oracle's site
   (http://www.oracle.com/technetwork/java/javase/downloads/index.html).

2. Install the Java `jdk-7u<version>-linux-x64.rpm` file on your CentOS machine using the following command:

   ```
   sudo rpm -ivh jdk-7u<version>-linux-x64.rpm
   ```

3. Add the following environment variable in the `~/.bashrc` file:

   ```
   export JAVA_HOME=/usr/java/jdk<version>
   ```

4. Add the path of the `bin` directory of the JDK to the `PATH` system environment variable to the `~/.bashrc` file:

   ```
   export PATH=$JAVA_HOME/bin:$PATH
   ```

5. Run the following command to reload the `bashrc` file on the current login terminal:

   ```
   source ~/.bashrc
   ```

6. Check the Java installation as follows:

   ```
   java -version
   ```

   The output of the preceding command is as follows:

   ```
   java version "1.7.0_71"
   Java(TM) SE Runtime Environment (build 1.7.0_71-b14)
   Java HotSpot(TM) 64-Bit Server VM (build 24.71-b01, mixed mode)
   ```

Deployment of the ZooKeeper cluster

In any distributed application, various processes need to coordinate with each other and share configuration information. ZooKeeper is an application that provides all these services in a reliable manner. Being a distributed application, Storm also uses a ZooKeeper cluster to coordinate various processes. All of the states associated with the cluster and the various tasks submitted to Storm are stored in ZooKeeper. This section describes how you can set up a ZooKeeper cluster. We will be deploying a ZooKeeper ensemble of three nodes that will handle one node failure. Following is the deployment diagram of the three node ZooKeeper ensemble:

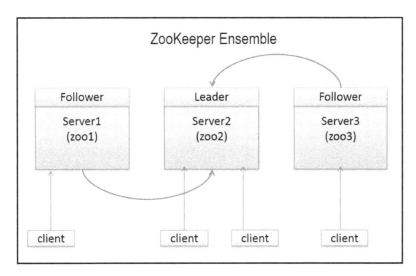

In the ZooKeeper ensemble, one node in the cluster acts as the leader, while the rest are followers. If the leader node of the ZooKeeper cluster dies, then an election for the new leader takes places among the remaining live nodes, and a new leader is elected. All write requests coming from clients are forwarded to the leader node, while the follower nodes only handle the read requests. Also, we can't increase the write performance of the ZooKeeper ensemble by increasing the number of nodes because all write operations go through the leader node.

It is advised to run an odd number of ZooKeeper nodes, as the ZooKeeper cluster keeps working as long as the majority (the number of live nodes is greater than $n/2$, where n being the number of deployed nodes) of the nodes are running. So if we have a cluster of four ZooKeeper nodes ($3 > 4/2$; only one node can die), then we can handle only one node failure, while if we had five nodes ($3 > 5/2$; two nodes can die) in the cluster, then we can handle two node failures.

Steps 1 to 4 need to be performed on each node to deploy the ZooKeeper ensemble:

1. Download the latest stable ZooKeeper release from the ZooKeeper site
   (`http://zookeeper.apache.org/releases.html`). At the time of writing, the
   latest version is ZooKeeper 3.4.6.

2. Once you have downloaded the latest version, unzip it. Now, we set up the
   `ZK_HOME` environment variable to make the setup easier.

3. Point the `ZK_HOME` environment variable to the unzipped directory. Create the
   configuration file, `zoo.cfg`, at the `$ZK_HOME/conf` directory using the following
   commands:

   ```
   cd $ZK_HOME/conf
   touch zoo.cfg
   ```

4. Add the following properties to the `zoo.cfg` file:

   ```
   tickTime=2000
   dataDir=/var/zookeeper
   clientPort=2181
   initLimit=5
   syncLimit=2
   server.1=zoo1:2888:3888
   server.2=zoo2:2888:3888
   server.3=zoo3.2888.3888
   ```

   Here, `zoo1`, `zoo2`, and `zoo3` are the IP addresses of the ZooKeeper nodes. The
   following are the definitions for each of the properties:

   - `tickTime`: This is the basic unit of time in milliseconds used by
     ZooKeeper. It is used to send heartbeats, and the minimum session
     timeout will be twice the `tickTime` value.
   - `dataDir`: This is the directory to store the in-memory database
     snapshots and transactional log.
   - `clientPort`: This is the port used to listen to client connections.
   - `initLimit`: This is the number of `tickTime` values needed to
     allow followers to connect and sync to a leader node.
   - `syncLimit`: This is the number of `tickTime` values that a follower
     can take to sync with the leader node. If the sync does not happen
     within this time, the follower will be dropped from the ensemble.

The last three lines of the `server.id=host:port:port` format specify that there are three nodes in the ensemble. In an ensemble, each ZooKeeper node must have a unique ID number between 1 and 255. This ID is defined by creating a file named `myid` in the `dataDir` directory of each node. For example, the node with the ID 1 (`server.1=zoo1:2888:3888`) will have a `myid` file at directory `/var/zookeeper` with `text 1` inside it.

For this cluster, create the `myid` file at three locations, shown as follows:

```
At zoo1 /var/zookeeper/myid contains 1
At zoo2 /var/zookeeper/myid contains 2
At zoo3 /var/zookeeper/myid contains 3
```

5. Run the following command on each machine to start the ZooKeeper cluster:

```
bin/zkServer.sh start
```

Check the status of the ZooKeeper nodes by performing the following steps:

6. Run the following command on the `zoo1` node to check the first node's status:

```
bin/zkServer.sh status
```

The following information is displayed:

```
JMX enabled by default
Using config: /home/root/zookeeper-3.4.6/bin/../conf/zoo.cfg
Mode: follower
```

The first node is running in `follower` mode.

7. Check the status of the second node by performing the following command:

```
bin/zkServer.sh status
```

The following information is displayed:

```
JMX enabled by default
Using config: /home/root/zookeeper-3.4.6/bin/../conf/zoo.cfg
Mode: leader
```

The second node is running in `leader` mode.

8. Check the status of the third node by performing the following command:

```
bin/zkServer.sh status
```

The following information is displayed:

```
JMX enabled by default
Using config: /home/root/zookeeper-3.4.6/bin/../conf/zoo.cfg
Mode: follower
```

The third node is running in `follower` mode.

9. Run the following command on the leader machine to stop the leader node:

```
bin/zkServer.sh stop
```

Now, check the status of the remaining two nodes by performing the following steps:

10. Check the status of the first node using the following command:

```
bin/zkServer.sh status
```

The following information is displayed:

```
JMX enabled by default
Using config: /home/root/zookeeper-3.4.6/bin/../conf/zoo.cfg
Mode: follower
```

The first node is again running in `follower` mode.

11. Check the status of the second node using the following command:

```
bin/zkServer.sh status
```

The following information is displayed:

```
JMX enabled by default
Using config: /home/root/zookeeper-3.4.6/bin/../conf/zoo.cfg
Mode: leader
```

The third node is elected as the new leader.

12. Now, restart the third node with the following command:

```
bin/zkServer.sh status
```

This was a quick introduction to setting up ZooKeeper that can be used for development; however, it is not suitable for production. For a complete reference on ZooKeeper administration and maintenance, please refer to the online documentation at the ZooKeeper site at `http://zookeeper.apache.org/doc/trunk/zookeeperAdmin.html`.

Setting up the Storm cluster

In this chapter, we will learn how to set up a three nodes Storm cluster, of which one node will be the active master node (Nimbus) and the other two will be worker nodes (supervisors).

The following is the deployment diagram of our three node Storm cluster:

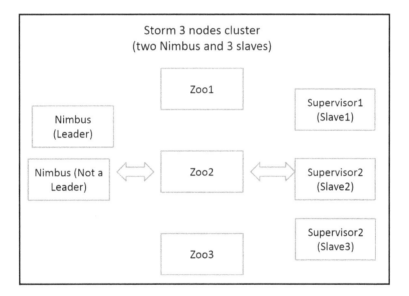

The following are the steps that need to be performed to set up a three node Storm cluster:

1. Install and run the ZooKeeper cluster. The steps for installing ZooKeeper are mentioned in the previous section.
2. Download the latest stable Storm release from `https://storm.apache.org/downloads.html`; at the time of writing, the latest version is Storm 1.0.2.

3. Once you have downloaded the latest version, copy and unzip it in all three machines. Now, we will set the $STORM_HOME environment variable on each machine to make the setup easier. The $STORM_HOME environment contains the path of the Storm home folder (for example, export STORM_HOME=/home/user/storm-1.0.2).

4. Go to the $STORM_HOME/conf directory in the master nodes and add the following lines to the storm.yaml file:

```
storm.zookeeper.servers:
 - "zoo1"
 - "zoo2"
 - "zoo3"
storm.zookeeper.port: 2181
nimbus.seeds: "nimbus1,nimbus2"
storm.local.dir: "/tmp/storm-data"
```

We are installing two master nodes.

5. Go to the $STORM_HOME/conf directory at each worker node and add the following lines to the storm.yaml file:

```
storm.zookeeper.servers:
 - "zoo1"
 - "zoo2"
 - "zoo3"
storm.zookeeper.port: 2181
nimbus.seeds: "nimbus1,nimbus2"
storm.local.dir: "/tmp/storm-data"
supervisor.slots.ports:
 - 6700
 - 6701
 - 6702
 - 6703
```

If you are planning to execute the Nimbus and supervisor on the same machine, then add the supervisor.slots.ports property to the Nimbus machine too.

6. Go to the $STORM_HOME directory at the master nodes and execute the following command to start the master daemon:

```
$> bin/storm nimbus &
```

7. Go to the $STORM_HOME directory at each worker node (or supervisor node) and execute the following command to start the worker daemons:

```
$> bin/storm supervisor &
```

Developing the hello world example

Before starting the development, you should have Eclipse and Maven installed in your project. The sample topology explained here will cover how to create a basic Storm project, including a spout and bolt, and how to build, and execute them.

Create a Maven project by using com.stormadvance as groupId and storm-example as artifactId.

Add the following Maven dependencies to the pom.xml file:

```
<dependency>
  <groupId>org.apache.storm</groupId>
  <artifactId>storm-core</artifactId>
  <version>1.0.2</version>
  <scope>provided<scope>
</dependency>
```

> Make sure the scope of the Storm dependency is provided, otherwise you will not be able to deploy the topology on the Storm cluster.

Add the following Maven build plugins in the pom.xml file:

```
<build>
  <plugins>
    <plugin>
      <artifactId>maven-assembly-plugin</artifactId>
      <version>2.2.1</version>
      <configuration>
        <descriptorRefs>
          <descriptorRef>jar-with-dependencies
          </descriptorRef>
```

```
            </descriptorRefs>
            <archive>
              <manifest>
                <mainClass />
              </manifest>
            </archive>
          </configuration>
          <executions>
            <execution>
              <id>make-assembly</id>
              <phase>package</phase>
              <goals>
                <goal>single</goal>
              </goals>
            </execution>
          </executions>
        </plugin>
      </plugins>
    </build>
```

Write your first sample spout by creating a `SampleSpout` class in the
`com.stormadvance.storm_example` package. The `SampleSpout` class extends the
serialized `BaseRichSpout` class. This spout does not connect to an external source to fetch
data, but randomly generates the data and emits a continuous stream of records. The
following is the source code of the `SampleSpout` class with an explanation:

```
public class SampleSpout extends BaseRichSpout {
  private static final long serialVersionUID = 1L;

  private static final Map<Integer, String> map = new HashMap<Integer,
String>();
  static {
    map.put(0, "google");
    map.put(1, "facebook");
    map.put(2, "twitter");
    map.put(3, "youtube");
    map.put(4, "linkedin");
  }
  private SpoutOutputCollector spoutOutputCollector;

  public void open(Map conf, TopologyContext context, SpoutOutputCollector
spoutOutputCollector) {
    // Open the spout
    this.spoutOutputCollector = spoutOutputCollector;
  }

  public void nextTuple() {
```

```
      // Storm cluster repeatedly calls this method to emita continuous
      // stream of tuples.
      final Random rand = new Random();
      // generate the random number from 0 to 4.
      int randomNumber = rand.nextInt(5);
      spoutOutputCollector.emit(new Values(map.get(randomNumber)));
      try{
        Thread.sleep(5000);
      }catch(Exception e) {
        System.out.println("Failed to sleep the thread");
      }
    }

  public void declareOutputFields(OutputFieldsDeclarer declarer) {

  // emit the tuple with field "site"
  declarer.declare(new Fields("site"));
  }
}
```

Write your first sample bolt by creating a SampleBolt class within the same package. The SampleBolt class extends the serialized BaseRichBolt class. This bolt will consume the tuples emitted by the SampleSpout spout and will print the value of the field site on the console. The following is the source code of the SampleStormBolt class with an explanation:

```
public class SampleBolt extends BaseBasicBolt {
  private static final long serialVersionUID = 1L;

  public void execute(Tuple input, BasicOutputCollector collector) {
    // fetched the field "site" from input tuple.
    String test = input.getStringByField("site");
    // print the value of field "site" on console.
    System.out.println("######### Name of input site is : " + test);
  }

  public void declareOutputFields(OutputFieldsDeclarer declarer) {
  }
}
```

Create a main `SampleStormTopology` class within the same package. This class creates an instance of the spout and bolt along with the classes, and chaines them together using a `TopologyBuilder` class. This class uses `org.apache.storm.LocalCluster` to simulate the Storm cluster. The `LocalCluster` mode is used for debugging/testing the topology on a developer machine before deploying it on the Storm cluster. The following is the implementation of the main class:

```
public class SampleStormTopology {
  public static void main(String[] args) throws AlreadyAliveException,
InvalidTopologyException {
    // create an instance of TopologyBuilder class
    TopologyBuilder builder = new TopologyBuilder();
    // set the spout class
    builder.setSpout("SampleSpout", new SampleSpout(), 2);
    // set the bolt class
    builder.setBolt("SampleBolt", new SampleBolt(),
4).shuffleGrouping("SampleSpout");
    Config conf = new Config();
    conf.setDebug(true);
    // create an instance of LocalCluster class for
    // executing topology in local mode.
    LocalCluster cluster = new LocalCluster();
    // SampleStormTopology is the name of submitted topology
    cluster.submitTopology("SampleStormTopology", conf,
builder.createTopology());
    try {
      Thread.sleep(100000);
    } catch (Exception exception) {
      System.out.println("Thread interrupted exception : " + exception);
    }
    // kill the SampleStormTopology
    cluster.killTopology("SampleStormTopology");
    // shutdown the storm test cluster
    cluster.shutdown();
  }
}
```

Go to your project's home directory and run the following commands to execute the topology in local mode:

```
$> cd $STORM_EXAMPLE_HOME
$> mvn compile exec:java -Dexec.classpathScope=compile -
Dexec.mainClass=com.stormadvance.storm_example.SampleStormTopology
```

Now create a new topology class for deploying the topology on an actual Storm cluster. Create a main `SampleStormClusterTopology` class within the same package. This class also creates an instance of the spout and bolt along with the classes, and chains them together using a `TopologyBuilder` class:

```
public class SampleStormClusterTopology {
  public static void main(String[] args) throws AlreadyAliveException,
InvalidTopologyException {
    // create an instance of TopologyBuilder class
    TopologyBuilder builder = new TopologyBuilder();
    // set the spout class
    builder.setSpout("SampleSpout", new SampleSpout(), 2);
    // set the bolt class
    builder.setBolt("SampleBolt", new SampleBolt(),
4).shuffleGrouping("SampleSpout");
    Config conf = new Config();
    conf.setNumWorkers(3);
    // This statement submit the topology on remote
    // args[0] = name of topology
    try {
      StormSubmitter.submitTopology(args[0], conf,
builder.createTopology());
    } catch (AlreadyAliveException alreadyAliveException) {
      System.out.println(alreadyAliveException);
    } catch (InvalidTopologyException invalidTopologyException) {
      System.out.println(invalidTopologyException);
    } catch (AuthorizationException e) {
      // TODO Auto-generated catch block
      e.printStackTrace();
    }
  }
}
```

Build your Maven project by running the following command on the projects home directory:

mvn clean install

The output of the preceding command is as follows:

```
          ------------------------------------------------------------ ----
  -
      [INFO] ------------------------------------------------------------ ----
  -
      [INFO] BUILD SUCCESS
      [INFO] ------------------------------------------------------------ ----
  -
      [INFO] Total time: 58.326s
```

```
[INFO] Finished at:
[INFO] Final Memory: 14M/116M
[INFO] ------------------------------------------------------------ ----
```

We can deploy the topology to the cluster using the following Storm client command:

```
bin/storm jar jarName.jar [TopologyMainClass] [Args]
```

The preceding command runs `TopologyMainClass` with the arguments `arg1` and `arg2`. The main function of `TopologyMainClass` is to define the topology and submit it to the Nimbus machine. The `storm jar` part takes care of connecting to the Nimbus machine and uploading the JAR part.

Log in on a Storm Nimbus machine and execute the following commands:

```
$> cd $STORM_HOME
$> bin/storm jar ~/storm_example-0.0.1-SNAPSHOT-jar-with-dependencies.jar
com.stormadvance.storm_example.SampleStormClusterTopology storm_example
```

In the preceding code `~/storm_example-0.0.1-SNAPSHOT-jar-with-dependencies.jar` is the path of the `SampleStormClusterTopology` JAR that we are deploying on the Storm cluster.

The following information is displayed:

```
702   [main] INFO  o.a.s.StormSubmitter - Generated ZooKeeper secret payload
for MD5-digest: -8367952358273199959:-5050558042400210383
793   [main] INFO  o.a.s.s.a.AuthUtils - Got AutoCreds []
856   [main] INFO  o.a.s.StormSubmitter - Uploading topology jar
/home/USER/storm_example-0.0.1-SNAPSHOT-jar-with-dependencies.jar to
assigned location: /tmp/storm-data/nimbus/inbox/stormjar-d3007821-
f87d-48af-8364-cff7abf8652d.jar
867   [main] INFO  o.a.s.StormSubmitter - Successfully uploaded topology jar
to assigned location: /tmp/storm-data/nimbus/inbox/stormjar-d3007821-
f87d-48af-8364-cff7abf8652d.jar
868   [main] INFO  o.a.s.StormSubmitter - Submitting topology storm_example
in distributed mode with conf
{"storm.zookeeper.topology.auth.scheme":"digest","storm.zookeeper.topology.
auth.payload":"-8367952358273199959:-5050558042400210383","topology.workers
":3}
  1007 [main] INFO  o.a.s.StormSubmitter - Finished submitting topology:
storm_example
```

Run the `jps` command to see the number of running JVM processes as follows:

```
jps
```

The preceding command's output is:

```
26827 worker
26530 supervisor
26824 worker
26468 nimbus
26822 worker
```

In the preceding code, a `worker` is the JVM launched for the `SampleStormClusterTopology` topology.

The different options of the Storm topology

This section covers the following operations that a user can perform on the Storm cluster:

- Deactivate
- Activate
- Rebalance
- Kill
- Dynamic log level settings

Deactivate

Storm supports the deactivating a topology. In the deactivated state, spouts will not emit any new tuples into the pipeline, but the processing of the already emitted tuples will continue. The following is the command to deactivate the running topology:

```
$> bin/storm deactivate topologyName
```

Deactivate `SampleStormClusterTopology` using the following command:

```
bin/storm deactivate SampleStormClusterTopology
```

The following information is displayed:

```
0 [main] INFO backtype.storm.thrift - Connecting to Nimbus at
localhost:6627
76 [main] INFO backtype.storm.command.deactivate - Deactivated topology:
SampleStormClusterTopology
```

Activate

Storm also the supports activating a topology. When a topology is activated, spouts will again start emitting tuples. The following is the command to activate the topology:

```
$> bin/storm activate topologyName
```

Activate SampleStormClusterTopology using the following command:

```
bin/storm activate SampleStormClusterTopology
```

The following information is displayed:

```
0 [main] INFO backtype.storm.thrift - Connecting to Nimbus at
localhost:6627
65 [main] INFO backtype.storm.command.activate - Activated topology:
SampleStormClusterTopology
```

Rebalance

The process of updating a the topology parallelism at the runtime is called a **rebalance**. A more detailed information of this operation acn be in Chapter 3, *Storm Parallelism and Data Partitioning*.

Kill

Storm topologies are never-ending processes. To stop a topology, we need to kill it. When killed, the topology first enters into the deactivation state, processes all the tuples already emitted into it, and then stops. Run the following command to kill SampleStormClusterTopology:

```
$> bin/storm kill SampleStormClusterTopology
```

The following information is displayed:

```
0 [main] INFO backtype.storm.thrift - Connecting to Nimbus at
localhost:6627
80 [main] INFO backtype.storm.command.kill-topology - Killed topology:
SampleStormClusterTopology
```

Now, run the `jps` command again to see the remaining JVM processes as follows:

```
jps
```

The preceding command's output is:

```
26530 supervisor
27193 Jps
26468 nimbus
```

Dynamic log level settings

This allows the user to change the log level of topology on runtime without stopping the topology. The detailed information of this operation can be found at the end of this chapter.

Walkthrough of the Storm UI

This section will show you how we can start the Storm UI daemon. However, before starting the Storm UI daemon, we assume that you have a running Storm cluster. The Storm cluster deployment steps are mentioned in the previous sections of this chapter. Now, go to the Storm home directory (`cd $STORM_HOME`) at the leader Nimbus machine and run the following command to start the Storm UI daemon:

```
$> cd $STORM_HOME
$> bin/storm ui &
```

By default, the Storm UI starts on the `8080` port of the machine where it is started. Now, we will browse to the `http://nimbus-node:8080` page to view the Storm UI, where Nimbus node is the IP address or hostname of the the Nimbus machine.

The following is a screenshot of the Storm home page:

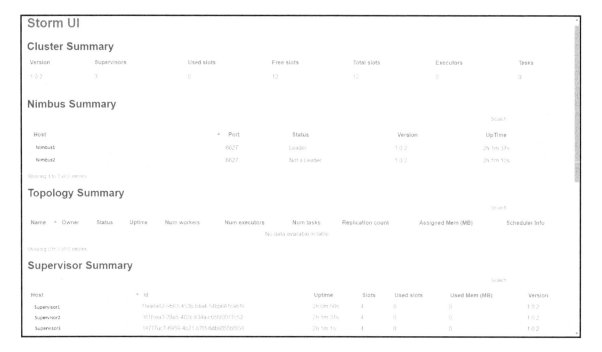

Cluster Summary section

This portion of the Storm UI shows the version of Storm deployed in the cluster, the uptime of the Nimbus nodes, number of free worker slots, number of used worker slots, and so on. While submitting a topology to the cluster, the user first needs to make sure that the value of the **Free slots** column should not be zero; otherwise, the topology doesn't get any worker for processing and will wait in the queue until a workers becomes free.

Nimbus Summary section

This portion of the Storm UI shows the number of Nimbus processes that are running in a Storm cluster. The section also shows the status of the Nimbus nodes. A node with the status `Leader` is an active master while the node with the status `Not a Leader` is a passive master.

Supervisor Summary section

This portion of the Storm UI shows the list of supervisor nodes running in the cluster, along with their **Id**, **Host**, **Uptime**, **Slots**, and **Used slots** columns.

Nimbus Configuration section

This portion of the Storm UI shows the configuration of the Nimbus node. Some of the important properties are:

- supervisor.slots.ports
- storm.zookeeper.port
- storm.zookeeper.servers
- storm.zookeeper.retry.interval
- worker.childopts
- supervisor.childopts

The following is a screenshot of **Nimbus Configuration**:

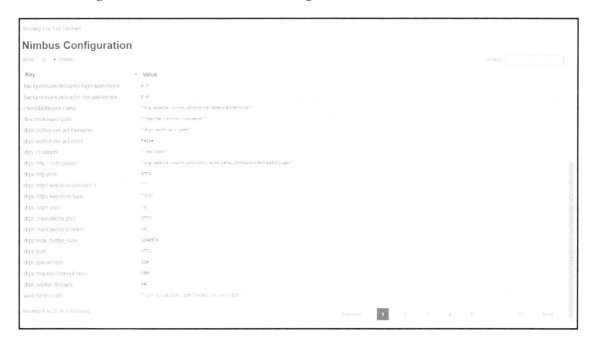

Topology Summary section

This portion of the Storm UI shows the list of topologies running in the Storm cluster, along with their ID, the number of workers assigned to the topology, the number of executors, number of tasks, uptime, and so on.

Let's deploy the sample topology (if it is not running already) in a remote Storm cluster by running the following command:

```
$> cd $STORM_HOME
$> bin/storm jar ~/storm_example-0.0.1-SNAPSHOT-jar-with-dependencies.jar
com.stormadvance.storm_example.SampleStormClusterTopology storm_example
```

We have created the `SampleStormClusterTopology` topology by defining three worker processes, two executors for `SampleSpout`, and four executors for `SampleBolt`.

After submitting `SampleStormClusterTopology` on the Storm cluster, the user has to refresh the Storm home page.

The following screenshot shows that the row is added for `SampleStormClusterTopology` in the **Topology Summary** section. The topology section contains the name of the topology, unique ID of the topology, status of the topology, uptime, number of workers assigned to the topology, and so on. The possible values of the **Status** fields are `ACTIVE`, `KILLED`, and `INACTIVE`.

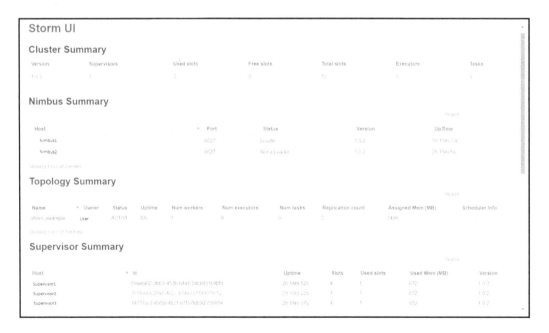

Let's click on `SampleStormClusterTopology` to view its detailed statistics. There are two screenshots for this. The first one contains the information about the number of workers, executors, and tasks assigned to the `SampleStormClusterTopology` topology:

The next screenshot contains information about the spouts and bolts, including the number of executors and tasks assigned to each spout and bolt:

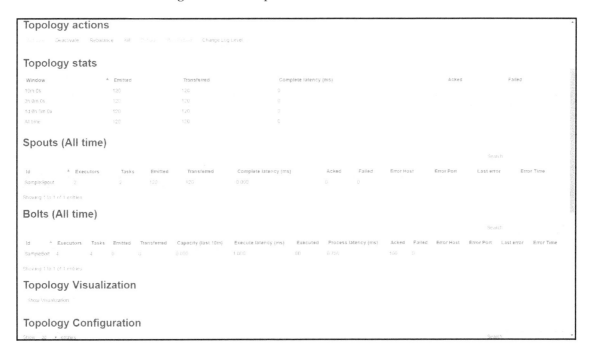

The information shown in the previous screenshots is as follows:

- **Topology stats**: This section will give information about the number of tuples emitted, transferred, and acknowledged, the capacity latency, and so on, within the windows of 10 minutes, 3 hours, 1 day, and since the start of the topology
- **Spouts (All time)**: This section shows the statistics of all the spouts running inside the topology
- **Bolts (All time)**: This section shows the statistics of all the bolts running inside the topology
- **Topology actions**: This section allows us to perform activate, deactivate, rebalance, kill, and other operations on the topologies directly through the Storm UI:
    - **Deactivate**: Click on **Deactivate** to deactivate the topology. Once the topology is deactivated, the spout stops emitting tuples and the status of the topology changes to **INACTIVE** on the Storm UI.

 Deactivating the topology does not free the Storm resource.

- **Activate**: Click on the **Activate** button to activate the topology. Once the topology is activated, the spout again starts emitting tuples.
- **Kill**: Click on the **Kill** button to destroy/kill the topology. Once the topology is killed, it will free all the Storm resources allotted to this topology. While killing the topology, the Storm will first deactivate the spouts and wait for the kill time mentioned on the alerts box so that the bolts have a chance to finish the processing of the tuples emitted by the spouts before the kill command. The following screenshot shows how we can kill the topology through the Storm UI:

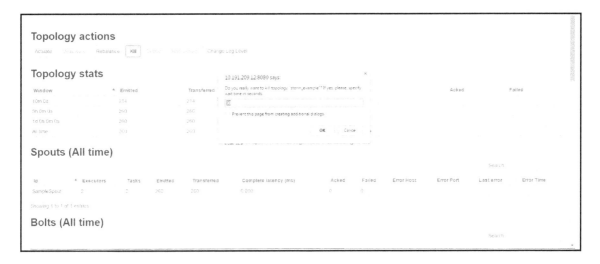

Let's go to the Storm UI's home page to check the status of `SampleStormClusterToplogy`, as shown in the following screenshot:

Dynamic log level settings

The dynamic log level allows us to change the log level setting of the topology on the runtime from the Storm CLI and the Storm UI.

Updating the log level from the Storm UI

Go through the following steps to update the log level from the Storm UI:

1. Deploy `SampleStormClusterTopology` again on the Storm cluster if it is not running.
2. Browse the Storm UI at `http://nimbus-node:8080/`.
3. Click on the `storm_example` topology.

4. Now click on the **Change Log Level** button to change the ROOT logger of the topology, as shown in the following are the screenshots:

5. Configure the entries mentioned in the following screenshots change the ROOT logger to **ERROR**:

6. If you are planning to change the logging level to **DEBUG**, then you must specify the timeout (expiry time) for that log level, as shown in the following screenshots:

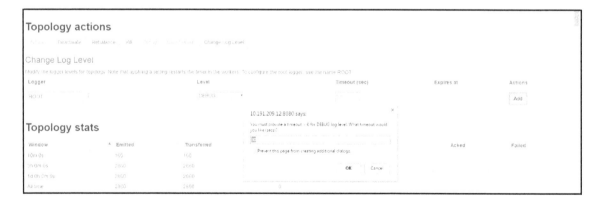

7. Once the time mentioned in the expiry time is reached, the log level will go back to the default value:

8. **Clear** button mentioned in the **Action** column will clear the log setting, and the application will set the default log setting again.

Updating the log level from the Storm CLI

We can modify the log level from the Storm CLI. The following is the command that the user has to execute from the Storm directory to update the log settings on the runtime:

```
bin/storm set_log_level [topology name] -l [logger name]=[LEVEL]:[TIMEOUT]
```

In the preceding code, topology name is the name of the topology, and logger name is the logger we want to change. If you want to change the ROOT logger, then use ROOT as a value of logger name. The LEVEL is the log level you want to apply. The possible values are DEBUG, INFO, ERROR, TRACE, ALL, WARN, FATAL, and OFF.

The TIMEOUT is the time in seconds. The log level will go back to normal after the timeout time. The value of TIMEOUT is mandatory if you are setting the log level to DEBUG/ALL.

The following is the command to change the log level setting for the storm_example topology:

```
$> bin/storm set_log_level storm_example -l ROOT=DEBUG:30
```

The following is the command to clear the log level setting:

```
$> ./bin/storm set_log_level storm_example -r ROOT
```

Summary

In this chapter, we have covered the installation of Storm and ZooKeeper clusters, the deployment of topologies on Storm clusters, the high availability of Nimbus nodes, and topology monitoring through the Storm UI. We have also covered the different operations a user can perform on running topology. Finally, we focused on how we can change the log level of running topology.

In the next chapter, we will focus on the distribution of topologies on multiple Storm machines/nodes.

3
Storm Parallelism and Data Partitioning

In the first two chapters, we have covered the introduction to Storm, the installation of Storm, and developing a sample topology. In this chapter, we are focusing on distribution of the topology on multiple Storm machines/nodes. This chapter covers the following points:

- Parallelism of topology
- How to configure parallelism at the code level
- Different types of stream groupings in a Storm cluster
- Guaranteed message processing
- Tick tuple

Parallelism of a topology

Parallelism means the distribution of jobs on multiple nodes/instances where each instance can work independently and can contribute to the processing of data. Let's first look at the processes/components that are responsible for the parallelism of a Storm cluster.

Worker process

A Storm topology is executed across multiple supervisor nodes in the Storm cluster. Each of the nodes in the cluster can run one or more JVMs called **worker processes**, which are responsible for processing a part of the topology.

A worker process is specific to one of the specific topologies and can execute multiple components of that topology. If multiple topologies are being run at the same time, none of them will share any of the workers, thus providing some degree of isolation between topologies.

Executor

Within each worker process, there can be multiple threads executing parts of the topology. Each of these threads is called an **executor**. An executor can execute only one of the components, that is, any spout or bolt in the topology.

Each executor, being a single thread, can execute only tasks assigned to it serially. The number of executors defined for a spout or bolt can be changed dynamically while the topology is running, which means that you can easily control the degree of parallelism of various components in your topology.

Task

This is the most granular unit of task execution in Storm. Each task is an instance of a spout or bolt. When defining a Storm topology, you can specify the number of tasks for each spout and bolt. Once defined, the number of tasks cannot be changed for a component at runtime. Each task can be executed alone or with another task of the same type, or another instance of the same spout or bolt.

The following diagram depicts the relationship between a worker process, executors, and tasks. In the following diagram, there are two executors for each component, with each hosting a different number of tasks.

Also, as you can see, there are two executors and eight tasks defined for one component (each executor is hosting four tasks). If you are not getting enough performance out of this configuration, you can easily change the number of executors for the component to four or eight to increase performance and the tasks will be uniformly distributed between all executors of that component. The following diagrams show the relationship between executor, task, and worker:

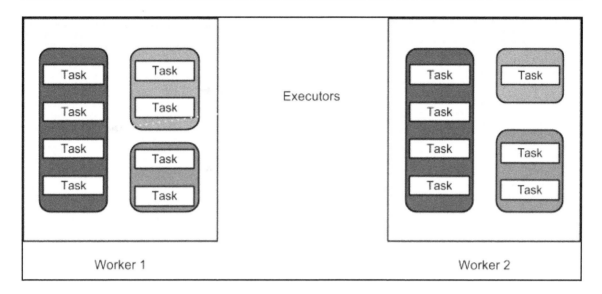

Configure parallelism at the code level

Storm provides an API to set the number of worker processes, number of executors, and number of tasks at the code level. The following section shows how we can configure parallelism at the code level.

We can set the number of worker processes at the code level by using the setNumWorkers method of the org.apache.storm.Config class. Here is the code snippet to show these settings in practice:

```
Config conf = new Config();
conf.setNumWorkers(3);
```

In the previous chapter, we configured the number of workers as three. Storm will assign the three workers for the SampleStormTopology and SampleStormClusterTopology topology.

We can set the number of executors at the code level by passing the `parallelism_hint` argument in the `setSpout(args,args,parallelism_hint)` or `setBolt(args,args,parallelism_hint)` methods of the `org.apache.storm.topology.TopologyBuilder` class. Here is the code snippet to show these settings in practice:

```
builder.setSpout("SampleSpout", new SampleSpout(), 2);
// set the bolt class
builder.setBolt("SampleBolt", new SampleBolt(),
4).shuffleGrouping("SampleSpout");
```

In the previous chapter, we set `parallelism_hint=2` for `SampleSpout` and `parallelism_hint=4` for `SampleBolt`. At the time of execution, Storm will assign two executors for `SampleSpout` and four executors for `SampleBolt`.

We can configure the number of tasks that can execute inside the executors. Here is the code snippet to show these settings in practice:

```
builder.setSpout("SampleSpout", new SampleSpout(), 2).setNumTasks(4);
```

In the preceding code, we have configured the two executors and four tasks of `SampleSpout`. For `SampleSpout`, Storm will assign two tasks per executor. By default, Storm will run one task per executor if the user does not set the number of tasks at the code level.

Worker process, executor, and task distribution

Let's assume the numbers of worker processes set for the topology is three, the number of executors for `SampleSpout` is three, and the number of executors for `SampleBolt` is three. Also, the number of tasks for `SampleBolt` is to be six, meaning that each `SampleBolt` executor will have two tasks. The following diagram shows what the topology would look like in operation:

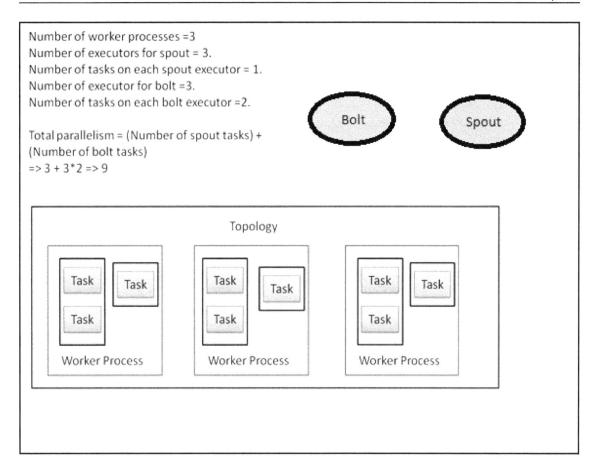

Rebalance the parallelism of a topology

As explained in the previous chapter, one of the key features of Storm is that it allows us to modify the parallelism of a topology at runtime. The process of updating a topology parallelism at runtime is called **rebalance**.

There are two ways to rebalance the topology:

- Using Storm Web UI
- Using Storm CLI

The Storm Web UI was covered in the previous chapter. This section covers how we can rebalance the topology using the Storm CLI tool. Here are the commands that we need to execute on Storm CLI to rebalance the topology:

```
> bin/storm rebalance [TopologyName] -n [NumberOfWorkers] -e
[Spout]=[NumberOfExecutos] -e [Bolt1]=[NumberOfExecutos]
[Bolt2]=[NumberOfExecutos]
```

The `rebalance` command will first deactivate the topology for the duration of the message timeout and then redistribute the workers evenly around the Storm cluster. After a few seconds or minutes, the topology will revert to the previous state of activation and restart the processing of input streams.

Rebalance the parallelism of a SampleStormClusterTopology topology

Let's first check the numbers of worker processes that are running in the Storm cluster by running the `jps` command on the supervisor machine:

Run the `jps` command on supervisor-1:

```
> jps
24347 worker
23940 supervisor
24593 Jps
24349 worker
```

Two worker processes are assigned to the supervisor-1 machine.

Now, run the `jps` command on supervisor-2:

```
> jps
24344 worker
23941 supervisor
24543 Jps
```

One worker process is assigned to the supervisor-2 machine.

A total of three worker processes are running on the Storm cluster.

Let's try reconfiguring `SampleStormClusterTopology` to use two worker processes, `SampleSpout` to use four executors, and `SampleBolt` to use four executors:

```
> bin/storm rebalance SampleStormClusterTopology -n 2 -e SampleSpout=4 -e
SampleBolt=4
0      [main] INFO  backtype.storm.thrift  - Connecting to Nimbus at
nimbus.host.ip:6627
58     [main] INFO  backtype.storm.command.rebalance  - Topology
SampleStormClusterTopology is rebalancing
```

Rerun the `jps` commands on the supervisor machines to view the number of worker processes.

Run the `jps` command on supervisor-1:

```
> jps
24377 worker
23940 supervisor
24593 Jps
```

Run the `jps` command on supervisor-2:

```
> jps
24353 worker
23941 supervisor
24543 Jps
```

In this case, two worker processes are shown previously. The first worker process is assigned to supervisor-1 and the other one is assigned to supervisor-2. The distribution of workers may vary depending on the number of topologies running on the system and the number of slots available on each supervisor. Ideally, Storm tries to distribute the load uniformly between all the nodes.

Different types of stream grouping in the Storm cluster

When defining a topology, we create a graph of computation with the number of bolt-processing streams. At a more granular level, each bolt executes multiple tasks in the topology. Thus, each task of a particular bolt will only get a subset of the tuples from the subscribed streams.

Stream grouping in Storm provides complete control over how this partitioning of tuples happens among the many tasks of a bolt subscribed to a stream. Grouping for a bolt can be defined on the instance of `org.apache.storm.topology.InputDeclarer` returned when defining bolts using the `org.apache`
`e.storm.topology.TopologyBuilder.setBolt` method.

Storm supports the following types of stream groupings.

Shuffle grouping

Shuffle grouping distributes tuples in a uniform, random way across the tasks. An equal number of tuples will be processed by each task. This grouping is ideal when you want to distribute your processing load uniformly across the tasks and where there is no requirement for any data-driven partitioning. This is one of the most commonly used groupings in Storm.

Field grouping

This grouping enables you to partition a stream on the basis of some of the fields in the tuples. For example, if you want all the tweets from a particular user to go to a single task, then you can partition the tweet stream using field grouping by username in the following manner:

```
builder.setSpout("1", new TweetSpout());
builder.setBolt("2", new TweetCounter()).fieldsGrouping("1", new
Fields("username"))
```

As a result of the field grouping being *hash (fields) % (no. of tasks)*, it does not guarantee that each of the tasks will get tuples to process. For example, if you have applied a field grouping on a field, say *X*, with only two possible values, *A* and *B*, and created two tasks for the bolt, then it might be possible that both *hash (A) % 2* and *hash (B) % 2* return equal values, which will result in all the tuples being routed to a single task and the other being completely idle.

Another common usage of field grouping is to join streams. Since partitioning happens solely on the basis of field values, and not the stream type, we can join two streams with any common join fields. The name of the fields needs not be the same. For example, in the order processing domain, we can join the `Order` stream and the `ItemScanned` stream to see when an order is completed:

```
builder.setSpout("1", new OrderSpout());
builder.setSpount("2", new ItemScannedSpout());
builder.setBolt("joiner", new OrderJoiner())
.fieldsGrouping("1", new Fields("orderId"))
.fieldsGrouping("2", new Fields("orderRefId"));
```

Since joins on streams vary from application to application, you'll make your own definition of a join, say joins over a time window, that can be achieved by composing field groupings.

All grouping

All grouping is a special grouping that does not partition the tuples but replicates them to all the tasks, that is, each tuple will be sent to each of the bolt's tasks for processing.

One common use case of all grouping is for sending signals to bolts. For example, if you are doing some kind of filtering on the streams, you can pass or change the filter parameters to all the bolts by sending them those parameters over a stream that is subscribed by all the bolt's tasks with an all grouping. Another example is to send a reset message to all the tasks in an aggregation bolt.

Global grouping

Global grouping does not partition the stream but sends the complete stream to the bolt's task, the smallest ID. A general use case of this is when there needs to be a reduce phase in your topology where you want to combine the results from previous steps in the topology into a single bolt.

Global grouping might seem redundant at first, as you can achieve the same results by defining the parallelism for the bolt as one if you only have one input stream. However, when you have multiple streams of data coming through a different path, you might want only one of the streams to be reduced and others to be parallel processes.

For example, consider the following topology. In this, you might want to combine all the tuples coming from **Bolt C** in a single **Bolt D** task, while you might still want parallelism for tuples coming from **Bolt E** to **Bolt D**:

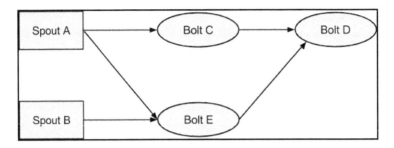

Direct grouping

In direct grouping, the emitter decides where each tuple will go for processing. For example, say we have a log stream and we want to process each log entry to be processed by a specific bolt task on the basis of the type of resource. In this case, we can use direct grouping.

Direct grouping can only be used with direct streams. To declare a stream as a direct stream, use the `backtype.storm.topology.OutputFieldsDeclarer.declareStream` method, which takes a `boolean` parameter. Once you have a direct stream to emit to, use `backtype.storm.task.OutputCollector.emitDirect` instead of emit methods to emit it. The `emitDirect` method takes a `taskId` parameter to specify the task. You can get the number of tasks for a component using the `backtype.storm.task.TopologyContext.getComponentTasks` method.

Local or shuffle grouping

If the tuple source and target bolt tasks are running in the same worker, using this grouping will act as a shuffle grouping only between the target tasks running on the same worker, thus minimizing any network hops, resulting in increased performance.

If there are no target bolt tasks running on the source worker process, this grouping will act similar to the shuffle grouping mentioned earlier.

None grouping

None grouping is used when you don't care about the way tuples are partitioned among various tasks. As of Storm 0.8, this is equivalent to using shuffle grouping.

Custom grouping

If none of the preceding groupings fit your use case, you can define your own custom grouping by implementing the `backtype.storm.grouping.CustomStreamGrouping` interface.

Here is a sample custom grouping that partitions the stream on the basis of the category in the tuples:

```java
public class CategoryGrouping implements CustomStreamGrouping, Serializable
{
  private static final Map<String, Integer> categories = ImmutableMap.of
  (
    "Financial", 0,
    "Medical", 1,
    "FMCG", 2,
    "Electronics", 3
  );

  private int tasks = 0;

  public void prepare(WorkerTopologyContext context, GlobalStreamId stream,
List<Integer> targetTasks)
  {
    tasks = targetTasks.size();
  }

  public List<Integer> chooseTasks(int taskId, List<Object> values) {
    String category = (String) values.get(0);
    return ImmutableList.of(categories.get(category) % tasks);
  }
}
```

The following diagram represents the Storm groupings graphically:

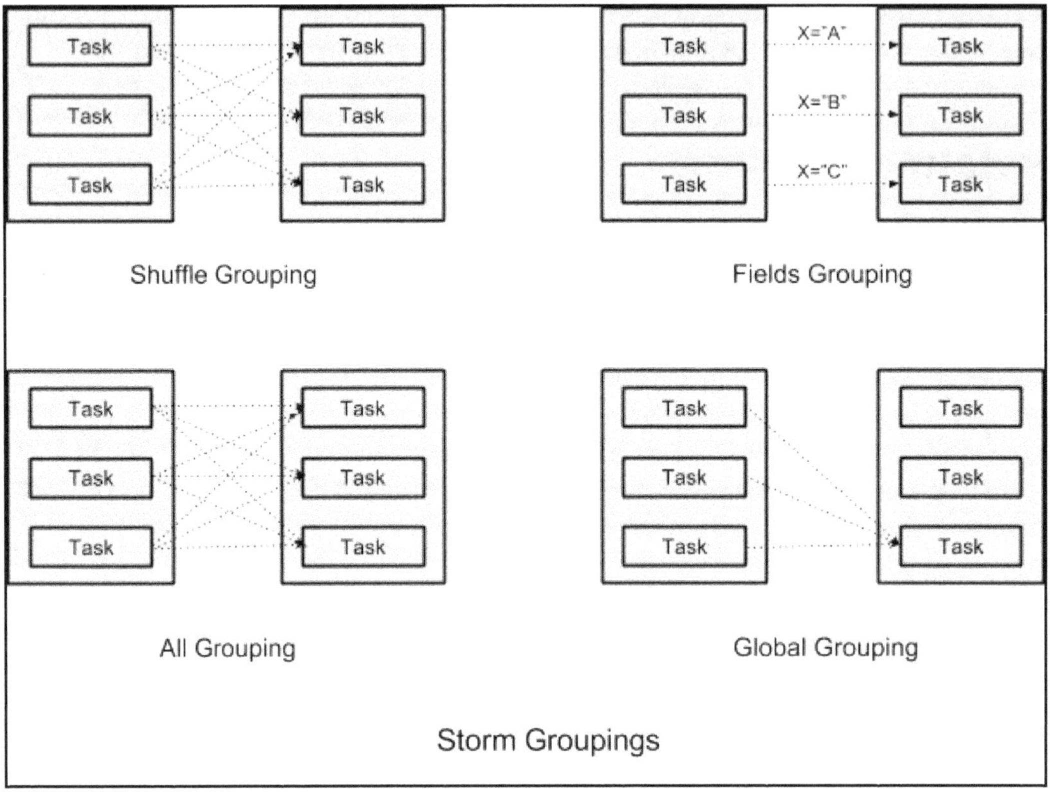

Storm Groupings

Guaranteed message processing

In a Storm topology, a single tuple being emitted by a spout can result in a number of tuples being generated in the later stages of the topology. For example, consider the following topology:

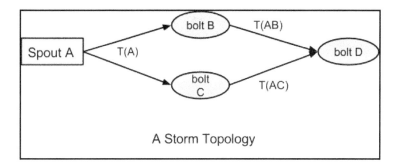

A Storm Topology

Here, **Spout A** emits a tuple **T(A)**, which is processed by **bolt B** and **bolt C**, which emit tuple **T(AB)** and **T(AC)** respectively. So, when all the tuples produced as a result of tuple **T(A)**--namely, the tuple tree **T(A)**, **T(AB)**, and **T(AC)**--are processed, we say that the tuple has been processed completely.

When some of the tuples in a tuple tree fail to process either due to some runtime error or a timeout that is configurable for each topology, then Storm considers that to be a failed tuple.

Here are the six steps that are required by Storm to guarantee message processing:

1. Tag each tuple emitted by a spout with a unique message ID. This can be done by using the `org.apache.storm.spout.SpoutOutputColletor.emit` method, which takes a `messageId` argument. Storm uses this message ID to track the state of the tuple tree generated by this tuple. If you use one of the emit methods that doesn't take a `messageId` argument, Storm will not track it for complete processing. When the message is processed completely, Storm will send an acknowledgement with the same `messageId` that was used while emitting the tuple.

2. A generic pattern implemented by spouts is that they read a message from a messaging queue, say RabbitMQ, produce the tuple into the topology for further processing, and then dequeue the message once it receives the acknowledgement that the tuple has been processed completely.

3. When one of the bolts in the topology needs to produce a new tuple in the course of processing a message, for example, **bolt B** in the preceding topology, then it should emit the new tuple anchored with the original tuple that it got from the spout. This can be done by using the overloaded emit methods in the `org.apache.storm.task.OutputCollector` class that takes an anchor tuple as an argument. If you are emitting multiple tuples from the same input tuple, then anchor each outgoing tuple.

4. Whenever you are done with processing a tuple in the execute method of your bolt, send an acknowledgment using the `org.apache.storm.task.OutputCollector.ack` method. When the acknowledgement reaches the emitting spout, you can safely mark the message as being processed and dequeue it from the message queue, if any.

5. Similarly, if there is some problem in processing a tuple, a failure signal should be sent back using the `org.apache.storm.task.OutputCollector.fail` method so that Storm can replay the failed message.

6. One of the general patterns of processing in Storm bolts is to process a tuple in, emit new tuples, and send an acknowledgement at the end of the execute method. Storm provides the `org.apache.storm.topology.base.BasicBasicBolt` class that automatically sends the acknowledgement at the end of the execute method. If you want to signal a failure, throw `org.apache.storm.topology.FailedException` from the execute method.

This model results in at-least-once message processing semantics, and your application should be ready to handle a scenario when some of the messages will be processed multiple times. Storm also provides exactly-once message processing semantics, which we will discuss in `Chapter 5`, *Trident Topology and Uses*.

Even though you can achieve some guaranteed message processing in Storm using the methods mentioned here, it is always a point to ponder whether you actually require it or not, as you can gain a large performance boost by risking some of the messages not being completely processed by Storm. This is a trade-off that you can think of when designing your application.

Tick tuple

In some use cases, a bolt needs to cache the data for a few seconds before performing some operation, such as cleaning the cache after every 5 seconds or inserting a batch of records into a database in a single request.

The tick tuple is the system-generated (Storm-generated) tuple that we can configure at each bolt level. The developer can configure the tick tuple at the code level while writing a bolt.

We need to overwrite the following method in the bolt to enable the tick tuple:

```
@Override
public Map<String, Object> getComponentConfiguration() {
  Config conf = new Config();
  int tickFrequencyInSeconds = 10;
  conf.put(Config.TOPOLOGY_TICK_TUPLE_FREQ_SECS,
  tickFrequencyInSeconds);
  return conf;
}
```

In the preceding code, we have configured the tick tuple time to 10 seconds. Now, Storm will start generating a tick tuple after every 10 seconds.

Also, we need to add the following code in the execute method of the bolt to identify the type of tuple:

```
@Override
public void execute(Tuple tuple) {
  if (isTickTuple(tuple)) {
    // now you can trigger e.g. a periodic activity
  }
  else {
    // do something with the normal tuple
  }
}

private static boolean isTickTuple(Tuple tuple) {
  return
  tuple.getSourceComponent().equals(Constants.SYSTEM_COMPONENT_ID) &&
tuple.getSourceStreamId().equals(Constants.SYSTEM_TICK_STREAM_ID);
}
```

If the output of the `isTickTuple()` method is true, then the input tuple is a tick tuple. Otherwise, it is a normal tuple emitted by the previous bolt.

Be aware that tick tuples are sent to bolts/spouts just like regular tuples, which means they will be queued behind other tuples that a bolt/spout is about to process via its `execute()` or `nextTuple()` method, respectively. As such, the time interval you configure for tick tuples is, in practice, served on a best-effort basis. For instance, if a bolt is suffering from high execution latency--for example, due to being overwhelmed by the incoming rate of regular, non-tick tuples--then you will observe that the periodic activities implemented in the bolt will get triggered later than expected.

Summary

In this chapter, we have shed some light on how we can define the parallelism of Storm, how we can distribute jobs between multiple nodes, and how we can distribute data between multiple instances of a bolt. The chapter also covered two important features: guaranteed message processing and the tick tuple.

In the next chapter, we are covering the Trident high-level abstraction over Storm. Trident is mostly used to solve the real-time transaction problem, which can't be solved through plain Storm.

4
Trident Introduction

In the previous chapters, we covered the architecture of Storm, its topology, bolts, spouts, tuples, and so on. In this chapter, we are covering Trident, which is a high-level abstraction over Storm.

We are covering the following points in this chapter:

- Introducing Trident
- Understanding Trident's data model
- Writing Trident functions, filters, and projections
- Trident repartitioning operations
- Trident aggregators
- When to use Trident

Trident introduction

Trident is a high-level abstraction built on top of Storm. Trident supports stateful stream processing, while pure Storm is a stateless processing framework. The main advantage of using Trident is that it guarantees that every message entered into the topology is processed only once, which would be difficult to achieve with vanilla Storm. The concept of Trident is similar to high-level batch processing tools, such as Cascading and Pig, developed over Hadoop. To achieve exactly-once processing, Trident processes the input stream in small batches. We will cover this in more detail in the Chapter 5, *Trident Topology and Uses*, *Trident state* section.

In the first three chapters, we learned that, in Storm's topology, the spout is the source of tuples. A tuple is a unit of data that can be processed by a Storm application, and a bolt is the processing powerhouse where we write the transformation logic. But in the Trident topology, the bolt is replaced with the higher level semantics of functions, aggregates, filters, and states.

Understanding Trident's data model

The Trident tuple is the data model of a Trident topology. The Trident tuple is the basic unit of data that can be processed by a Trident topology. Each tuple consists of a predefined list of fields. The value of each field can be a byte, char, integer, long, float, double, Boolean, or byte array. During the construction of a topology, operations are performed on a tuple, which will either add new fields to the tuple or replace the tuple with a new set of fields.

Each of the fields in a tuple can be accessed by name, (`getValueByField(String)`), or its positional index, (`getValue(int)`), in the tuple. The Trident tuple also provides convenience methods, such as `getIntegerByField(String)`, which saves you from typecasting the objects.

Writing Trident functions, filters, and projections

This section covers the definition of Trident functions, filters, and projections. Trident functions, filters, and projections are used to modify/filter the input tuples based on certain criteria. This section also covers how we can write Trident functions, filters, and projections.

Trident function

Trident functions contain logic to modify the original tuple. A Trident function gets a set of fields of the tuple as input and emits one or more tuples as output. The fields of the output tuples are merged with the fields of the input tuple to form the complete tuple, which will pass to the next action in the topology. If the Trident function emits no tuples corresponding to the input tuple, then that tuple is removed from the stream.

We can write a custom Trident function by extending the
`storm.trident.operation.BaseFunction` class and implementing the
`execute(TridentTuple tuple, TridentCollector collector)` method.

Let's write the sample Trident function, which will return the new field called `sum`:

```
public class SumFunction extends BaseFunction {

  private static final long serialVersionUID = 5L;

  public void execute(TridentTuple tuple, TridentCollector collector) {
    int number1 = tuple.getInteger(0);
    int number2 = tuple.getInteger(1);
    int sum = number1+number2;
    // emit the sum of first two fields
    collector.emit(new Values(sum));
  }
}
```

Suppose we get `dummyStream` as input, which contains four fields, a, b, c, d, and only fields
a and b are passed as input fields to the `SumFunction` function. The `SumFunction` class
emits new a field, `sum`. The `sum` field emitted by the `execute` method of the `SumFunction`
class is merged with the input tuple to form the complete tuple. Hence, the total number of
fields in the output tuple is 5 (a, b, c, d, sum). Here is a sample piece of code that
shows how we can pass the input fields and the name of the new field to the Trident
function:

```
dummyStream.each(new Fields("a","b"), new SumFunction (), new
Fields("sum"))
```

The following diagram shows the input tuples, `SumFunction`, and the output tuples. The
output tuples contain five fields, a, b, c, d, and sum:

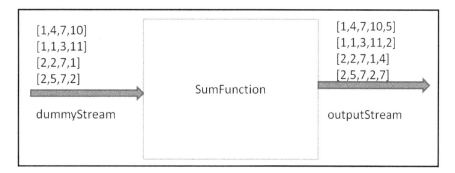

Trident filter

A Trident filter gets a set of fields as input and returns either true or false depending on whether a certain condition is satisfied or not. If true is returned, then the tuple is kept in the output stream; otherwise, the tuple is removed from the stream.

We can write a custom Trident filter by extending the `storm.trident.operation.BaseFilter` class and implementing the `isKeep(TridentTuple tuple)` method.

Let's write a sample Trident filter that will check whether the sum of the input fields is even or odd. If the sum is even, then the Trident filter emits true; otherwise it emits false:

```
public static class CheckEvenSumFilter extends BaseFilter{
  private static final long serialVersionUID = 7L;

  public boolean isKeep(TridentTuple tuple) {
    int number1 = tuple.getInteger(0);
    int number2 = tuple.getInteger(1);
    int sum = number1+number2;
    if(sum % 2 == 0) {
      return true;
    }
    return false;
  }
}
```

Suppose we get `dummyStream` as input, which contains four fields, a, b, c, d, and only fields a and b are passed as input fields to the `CheckEvenSumFilter` filter. The `execute` method of the `CheckEvenSumFilter` class will emit only those tuples whose sum of a and b is even. Here is a sample piece of code that shows how we can define the input fields for a Trident filter:

```
dummyStream.each(new Fields("a","b"), new CheckEvenSumFilter ())
```

The following diagram shows the input tuples, `CheckEvenSumFilter`, and output tuples. `outputStream` contains only those tuples whose sum of fields `a` and `b` is even:

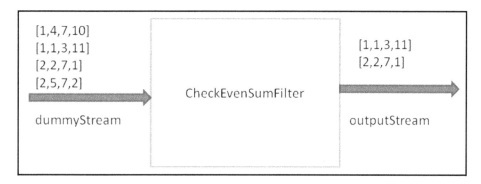

Trident projection

A Trident projection keeps only those fields in the stream that are specified in the projection operation. Suppose an input stream contains three fields, x, y, and z, and we are passing field x to the projection operation, then the output tuples will contain a single field, x. Here is the piece of code that shows how we can use the projection operation:

```
mystream.project(new Fields("x"))
```

The following diagram shows the Trident projection:

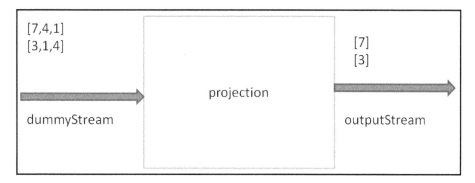

Trident repartitioning operations

By performing repartitioning operations, a user can partition tuples across multiple tasks. The repartitioning operation doesn't make any changes to the content of the tuples. Also, the tuples will only pass over the network for the repartitioning operation. Here are the different types of repartitioning operation.

Utilizing shuffle operation

This repartitioning operation partitions the tuples in a uniform, random way across multiple tasks. This repartitioning operation is generally used when we want to distribute the processing load uniformly across the tasks. The following diagram shows how the input tuples are repartitioned using the `shuffle` operation:

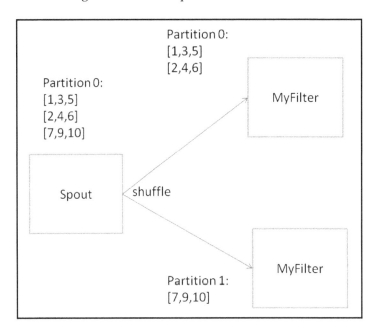

Here is a piece of code that shows how we can use the `shuffle` operation:

```
mystream.shuffle().each(new Fields("a","b"), new
myFilter()).parallelismHint(2)
```

Utilizing partitionBy operation

This repartitioning operation enables you to partition the stream on the basis of the fields in the tuples. For example, if you want all the tweets from a particular user to go to the same target partition, then you can partition the tweet stream by applying partitionBy to the username field in the following manner:

```
mystream.partitionBy(new Fields("username")).each(new
Fields("username","text"), new myFilter()).parallelismHint(2)
```

The partitionBy operation applies the following formula to decide the target partition:

Target Partition = hash(fields) % (number of target partition)

As the preceding formula shows, the partitionBy operation calculates the hash of the input fields to decide the target partition. Hence, it does not guarantee that all the tasks will get tuples to process. For example, if you have applied a partitionBy to a field, say X, with only two possible values, A and B, and created two tasks for the MyFilter filter, then it might be possible that hash (A) % 2 and hash (B) % 2 are equal, which will result in all the tuples being routed to a single task and the other tuples being completely idle.

The following diagram shows how the input tuples are repartitioned using the partitionBy operation:

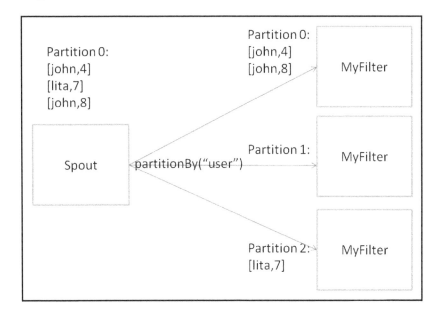

As the preceding diagram shows, **Partition 0** and **Partition 2** contain a set of tuples, but **Partition 1** is empty.

Utilizing global operation

This repartitioning operation routes all the tuples to the same partition. Hence, the same target partition is selected for all the batches in the stream. Here is a diagram that shows how the tuples are repartitioned using the `global` operation:

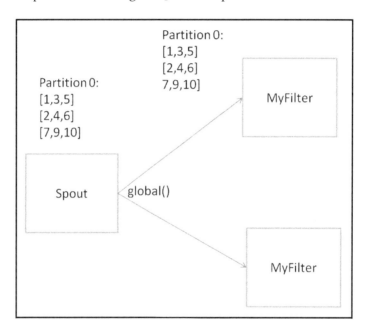

Here is a piece of code that shows how we can use the `global` operation:

```
mystream.global().each(new Fields("a","b"), new
myFilter()).parallelismHint(2)
```

Utilizing broadcast operation

The `broadcast` operation is a special repartitioning operation that does not partition the tuples, but replicates them to all partitions. Here is a diagram that shows how the tuples are sent over the network:

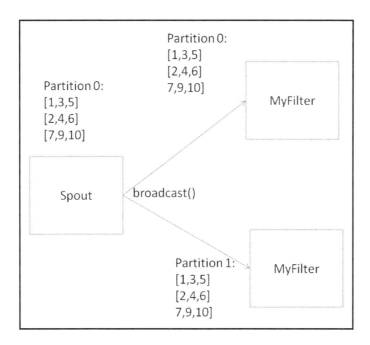

Here is a piece of code that shows how we can use the `broadcast` operation:

```
mystream.broadcast().each(new Fields("a","b"), new
myFilter()).parallelismHint(2)
```

Utilizing batchGlobal operation

This repartitioning operation sends all the tuples belonging to one batch into the same partition. The other batches of the same stream may go to a different partition. As the name suggests, this repartition is global at the batch level. Here is a diagram that shows how the tuples are repartitioned using the `batchGlobal` operation:

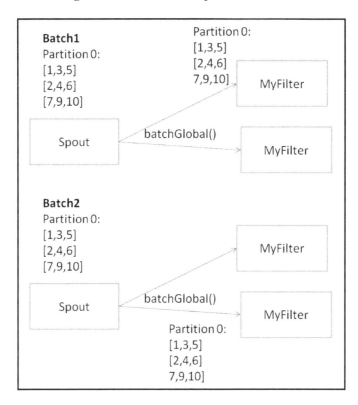

Here is a piece of code that shows how we can use the `batchGlobal` operation:

```
mystream.batchGlobal().each(new Fields("a","b"), new
myFilter()).parallelismHint(2)
```

Utilizing partition operation

If none of the preceding repartitioning fits your use case, you can define your own custom repartition function by implementing the `org.apche.storm.grouping.CustomStreamGrouping` interface.

Here is a sample custom repartition that partitions the stream on the basis of the value of the country field:

```
public class CountryRepartition implements CustomStreamGrouping,
Serializable {

  private static final long serialVersionUID = 1L;

  private static final Map<String, Integer> countries = ImmutableMap.of (
    "India", 0,
    "Japan", 1,
    "United State", 2,
    "China", 3,
    "Brazil", 4
  );
  private int tasks = 0;

  public void prepare(WorkerTopologyContext context, GlobalStreamId stream,
List<Integer> targetTasks)
    {
      tasks = targetTasks.size();
    }

  public List<Integer> chooseTasks(int taskId, List<Object> values) {
    String country = (String) values.get(0);
    return ImmutableList.of(countries.get(country) % tasks);
  }
}
```

The CountryRepartition class implements the `org.apache.storm.grouping.CustomStreamGrouping` interface. The `chooseTasks()` method contains the repartitioning logic to identify the next task in the topology for the input tuple. The `prepare()` method is called at the start and performs the initialization activity.

Trident aggregator

The Trident aggregator is used to perform the aggregation operation on the input batch, partition, or input stream. For example, if a user wants to count the number of tuples present in each batch, then we can use the count aggregator to count the number of tuples in each batch. The output of the aggregator completely replaces the value of the input tuple. There are three types of aggregator available in Trident:

- partitionAggregate
- aggregate
- persistenceAggregate

Let's understand each type of aggregator in detail.

partitionAggregate

As the name suggests, the partitionAggregate works on each partition instead of the whole batch. The output of partitionAggregate completely replaces the input tuple. Also, the output of partitionAggregate contains a single-field tuple. Here is a piece of code that shows how we can use partitionAggregate:

```
mystream.partitionAggregate(new Fields("x"), new Count() ,new new
Fields("count"))
```

For example, we get an input stream containing the fields x and y and we apply a partitionAggregate function to each partition; the output tuples contain a single field called count. The count field represent the number of tuples presents in the input partition:

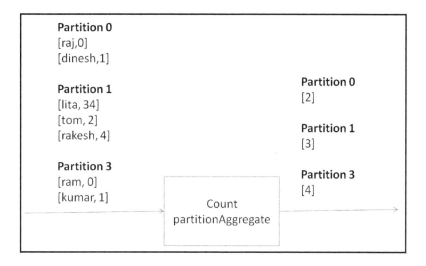

aggregate

The `aggregate` works on each batch. During the aggregate process, the tuples are first repartitioned using the global operation to combine all the partitions of the same batch into a single partition and then the aggregation function is run on each batch. Here is a piece of code that shows how we can use `aggregate`:

```
mystream.aggregate(new Fields("x"), new Count() ,new new Fields("count"))
```

There are three types of aggregator interface available in Trident:

- `ReducerAggregator`
- `Aggregator`
- `CombinerAggregator`

These three aggregator interfaces can also be used with `partitionAggregate`.

ReducerAggregator

The `ReducerAggregator` first runs the global repartitioning operation on the input stream to combine all the partitions of the same batch into a single partition, and then runs the aggregation function on each batch. The `ReducerAggregator<T>` interface contains the following methods:

- `init()`: This method returns the initial value
- `Reduce(T curr, TridentTuple tuple)`: This method iterates over the input tuples and emits a single tuple with a single value

This example shows how we can implement `Sum` using the `ReducerAggregator`:

```
public static class Sum implements ReducerAggregator<Long> {

  private static final long serialVersionUID = 1L;
  /** return the initial value zero
  */
  public Long init() {
    return 0L;
  }
  /** Iterates on the input tuples, calculate the sum and
  * produce the single tuple with single field as output.
  */
  public Long reduce(Long curr, TridentTuple tuple) {
    return curr+tuple.getLong(0);
  }
}
```

Aggregator

The `Aggregator` first runs the global repartitioning operation on the input stream to combine all the partitions of the same batch into a single partition, and then runs the aggregation function on each batch. By definition, the `Aggregator` looks very similar to the ReduceAggregator. The `BaseAggregator<State>` contains the following methods:

- `init(Object batchId, TridentCollector collector)`: The `init()` method is called before starting the processing of a batch. This method returns the `State` object, which will be used to save the state of the batch. This object is used by the `aggregate()` and `complete()` methods.

- aggregate (State s, TridentTuple tuple, TridentCollector collector): This method iterates over each tuple of a given batch. This method updates the state in the State object after processing each tuple.
- complete(State state, TridentCollector tridentCollector): This method is called at the end, if all the tuples of a given batch are processed. This method returns a single tuple corresponding to each batch.

Here is an example that shows how we can implement a sum using the BaseAggregator:

```
public static class SumAsAggregator extends
BaseAggregator<SumAsAggregator.State> {


  private static final long serialVersionUID = 1L;
  // state class
  static class State {
    long count = 0;
  }
  // Initialize the state
  public State init(Object batchId, TridentCollector collector) {
    return new State();
  }
  // Maintain the state of sum into count variable.
  public void aggregate(State state, TridentTuple tridentTuple,
TridentCollector tridentCollector) {
    state.count = tridentTuple.getLong(0) + state.count;
  }
  // return a tuple with single value as output
  // after processing all the tuples of given batch.
  public void complete(State state, TridentCollector tridentCollector) {
    tridentCollector.emit(new Values(state.count));
  }
}
```

CombinerAggregator

The CombinerAggregator first runs the partitionAggregate on each partition, then runs the global repartitioning operation to combine all the partitions of the same batch into a single partition, and then reruns the aggregator on the final partition to emit the desired output. The network transfer here is less compared to the other two aggregators. Hence, the overall performance of the CombinerAggregator is better than the Aggregator and ReduceAggregator.

The `CombinerAggregator<T>` interface contains the following methods:

- `init()`: This method runs on each input tuple to retrieve the fields' value from the tuple.
- `combine(T val1, T val2)`: This method combines the values of the tuples. This method emits a single tuple with a single field as the output.
- `zero()`: This method returns zero if the input partition contains no tuple.

This example shows how we can implement `Sum` using `CombinerAggregator`:

```
public class Sum implements CombinerAggregator<Number> {

  private static final long serialVersionUID = 1L;

  public Number init(TridentTuple tridentTuple) {
    return (Number) tridentTuple.getValue(0);
  }

  public Number combine(Number number1, Number number2) {
    return Numbers.add(number1, number2);
  }

  public Number zero() {
    return 0;
  }
}
```

persistentAggregate

The `persistentAggregate` works on all the tuples across all the batches in a stream and persists the aggregate result into the source of state (memory, Memcached, Cassandra, or some other database). Here is some code that shows how we can use the `persistentAggregate`:

```
mystream.persistentAggregate(new MemoryMapState.Factory(),new
Fields("select"),new Count(),new Fields("count"));
```

We will discuss in more detail in the Chapter 5, *Trident Topology and Uses*, *Trident state* section.

Aggregator chaining

Trident provides a feature to apply multiple aggregators to the same input stream, and this process is called **aggregator chaining**. Here is a piece of code that shows how we can use aggregator chaining:

```
mystream.chainedAgg()
        .partitionAggregate(new Fields("b"), new Average(), new
Fields("average"))
        .partitionAggregate(new Fields("b"), new Sum(), new Fields("sum"))
        .chainEnd();
```

We have applied the `Average()` and `Sum()` aggregators to each partition. The output of `chainedAgg()` contains a single tuple corresponding to each input partition. The output tuple contains two fields, `sum` and `average`.

The following diagram shows how aggregator chaining works:

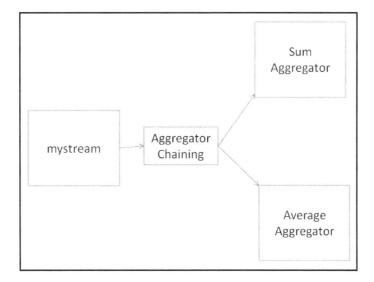

Utilizing the groupBy operation

The `groupBy` operation doesn't involve any repartitioning. The `groupBy` operation converts the input stream into a grouped stream. The main function of the `groupBy` operation is to modify the behavior of the subsequent aggregate function. The following diagram shows how the `groupBy` operation groups the tuples of a single partition:

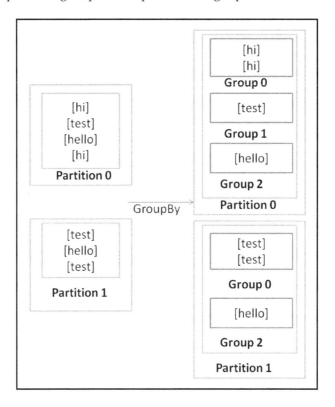

The behavior of `groupBy` is dependent on a position where it is used. The following behavior is possible:

- If the `groupBy` operation is used before a `partitionAggregate`, then the `partitionAggregate` will run the `aggregate` on each group created within the partition.
- If the `groupBy` operation is used before an `aggregate`, the tuples of the same batch are first repartitioned into a single partition, then `groupBy` is applied to each single partition, and at the end it will perform the `aggregate` operation on each group.

When to use Trident

It is very easy to achieve exactly-once processing using the Trident topology, and Trident was designed for this purpose. It would be difficult to achieve exactly-once processing with vanilla Storm, so Trident will be useful when we need exactly-once processing.

Trident is not fit for all use cases, especially for high-performance use cases, because Trident adds complexity to Storm and manages the state.

Summary

In this chapter, we mainly concentrated on Trident high-level abstraction over Storm and learned about the Trident filter, function, aggregator, and repartitioning operations.

In the next chapter, we will cover non-transactional topology, Trident topology, and Trident topology using a distributed RPC.

5
Trident Topology and Uses

In the previous chapter, we covered an overview of Trident. In this chapter, we are going to cover the development of a Trident topology. Here are the important points we are going to cover in this chapter:

- The Trident `groupBy` operation
- Non-transactional topology
- Trident hello world topology
- Trident state
- Distributed RPC
- When to use Trident

Trident groupBy operation

The groupBy operation doesn't involve any repartitioning. The groupBy operation converts the input stream into a grouped stream. The main function of the groupBy operation is to modify the behavior of subsequent aggregate functions.

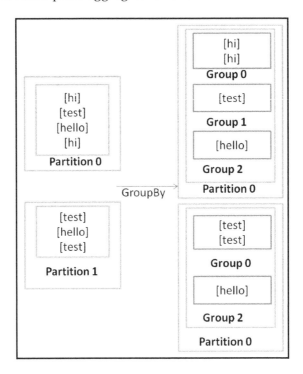

groupBy before partitionAggregate

If the groupBy operation is used before a partitionAggregate, then the partitionAggregate will run the aggregate on each group created within the partition.

groupBy before aggregate

If the groupBy operation is used before an aggregate, then input tuples is first repartition and then perform the aggregate operation on each group.

Non-transactional topology

In non-transactional topology, a spout emits a batch of tuples and doesn't guarantee what's in each batch. With a processing mechanism, we can divide the pipeline into two categories:

- **At-most-once-processing**: In this type of topology, failed tuples are not retried. Hence, the spout does not wait for an acknowledgment.
- **At-least-once-processing**: Failed tuples are retried in the processing pipeline. Hence, this type of topology guarantees that every tuple that enters the processing pipeline must be processed at least once.

We can write a non-transactional spout by implementing the `org.apache.storm.trident.spout.IBatchSpout` interface.

This example shows how we can write a Trident spout:

```
public class FakeTweetSpout implements IBatchSpout{

    private static final long serialVersionUID = 10L;
    private intbatchSize;
    private HashMap<Long, List<List<Object>>>batchesMap = new HashMap<Long,
List<List<Object>>>();
    public FakeTweetSpout(intbatchSize) {
        this.batchSize = batchSize;
    }
    private static final Map<Integer, String> TWEET_MAP = new
HashMap<Integer, String>();
    static {
        TWEET_MAP.put(0, "#FIFA worldcup");
        TWEET_MAP.put(1, "#FIFA worldcup");
        TWEET_MAP.put(2, "#FIFA worldcup");
        TWEET_MAP.put(3, "#FIFA worldcup");
        TWEET_MAP.put(4, "#Movie top 10");
    }
    private static final Map<Integer, String> COUNTRY_MAP = new
HashMap<Integer, String>();
    static {
        COUNTRY_MAP.put(0, "United State");
        COUNTRY_MAP.put(1, "Japan");
        COUNTRY_MAP.put(2, "India");
        COUNTRY_MAP.put(3, "China");
        COUNTRY_MAP.put(4, "Brazil");
    }
    private List<Object>recordGenerator() {
        final Random rand = new Random();
        intrandomNumber = rand.nextInt(5);
```

```
              int randomNumber2 = rand.nextInt(5);
              return new
      Values(TWEET_MAP.get(randomNumber),COUNTRY_MAP.get(randomNumber2));
          }
          public void ack(long batchId) {
              this.batchesMap.remove(batchId);
          }

          public void close() {
              // Here we should close all the external connections
          }

          public void emitBatch(long batchId, TridentCollector collector) {
              List<List<Object>> batches = this.batchesMap.get(batchId);
              if(batches == null) {
                  batches = new ArrayList<List<Object>>();;
                  for (inti=0;i<this.batchSize;i++) {
                      batches.add(this.recordGenerator());
                  }
                  this.batchesMap.put(batchId, batches);
              }
              for(List<Object>list : batches){
      collector.emit(list);
              }
          }

          public Map getComponentConfiguration() {
              // TODO Auto-generated method stub
              return null;
          }

          public Fields getOutputFields() {
              return new Fields("text","Country");
          }

          public void open(Map arg0, TopologyContext arg1) {
              // TODO Auto-generated method stub
          }

      }
```

The `FakeTweetSpout` class implements the
`org.apache.storm.trident.spout.IBatchSpout` interface. The construct of
`FakeTweetSpout(intbatchSize)` takes `batchSize` as an argument. If `batchSize` is 3,
then every batch emitted by `FakeTweetSpout` class contains three tuples. The
`recordGenerator` method contains logic to generate the fake tweet. Here is the sample
fake tweet:

```
["Adidas #FIFA World Cup Chant Challenge", "Brazil"]
["The Great Gatsby is such a good movie","India"]
```

The `getOutputFields` method returns two fields, `text` and `Country`. The
`emitBatch(long batchId, TridentCollector collector)` method uses the
`batchSize` variable to decide the number of tuples in each batch and emits a batch into the
processing pipeline.

The `batchesMap` collection contains `batchId` as a key and the batch of tuples as a value.
All the batches emitted by `emitBatch(long batchId, TridentCollector
collector)` will be added into `batchesMap`.

The `ack(long batchId)` method receives `batchId` as an acknowledgment, and will
remove the corresponding batch from `batchesMap`.

Trident hello world topology

This section explains how we can write a Trident hello world topology. Perform the
following steps to create Trident hello world topology:

1. Create a Maven project by using `com.stormadvance` as the `groupId` and
    `storm_trident` as the `artifactId`.
2. Add the following dependencies and repositories to the `pom.xml` file:

```
<dependencies>
<dependency>
        <groupId>junit</groupId>
        <artifactId>junit</artifactId>
        <version>3.8.1</version>
        <scope>test</scope>
</dependency>
<dependency>
        <groupId>org.apache.storm</groupId>
        <artifactId>storm-core</artifactId>
        <version>1.0.2</version>
```

```
           <scope>provided</scope>
       </dependency>
</dependencies>
```

3. Create a `TridentUtility` class in a `com.stormadvance.storm_trident` package. This class contains the Trident filter and function that we are going to use in the Trident hello world example:

```
public class TridentUtility {
    /**
     * Get the comma separated value as input, split the field by
comma, and
     * then emits multiple tuple as output.
     *
     */
    public static class Split extends BaseFunction {

            private static final long serialVersionUID = 2L;

            public void execute(TridentTuple tuple, TridentCollector
collector) {
                    String countries = tuple.getString(0);
                    for (String word :countries.split(",")) {
                            // System.out.println("word -"+word);
                            collector.emit(new Values(word));
                    }
            }
    }

    /**
     * This class extends BaseFilter and contain isKeep method which
emits only
     * those tuple which has #FIFA in text field.
     */
    public static class TweetFilter extends BaseFilter {

            private static final long serialVersionUID = 1L;

            public booleanisKeep(TridentTuple tuple) {
                    if (tuple.getString(0).contains("#FIFA")) {
                            return true;
                    } else {
                            return false;
                    }
            }
    }

}
```

```
/**
 * This class extends BaseFilter and contain isKeep method which
will print
 * the input tuple.
 *
 */
public static class Print extends BaseFilter {

        private static final long serialVersionUID = 1L;

        public booleanisKeep(TridentTuple tuple) {
                System.out.println(tuple);
                return true;
        }


}
}
```

The `TridentUtility` class contains three inner classes: `Split`, `TweetFilter`, and `Print`.

The `Split` class extends the `org.apache.storm.trident.operation.BaseFunction` class and contains the `execute(TridentTuple tuple, TridentCollector collector)` method. The `execute()` method takes comma-separated values as input, splits the input value, and emits multiple tuples as output.

The `TweetFilter` class extends the `org.apache.storm.trident.operation.BaseFilter` class and contains the `isKeep(TridentTuple tuple)` method. The `isKeep()` method takes a tuple as its input and checks whether the input tuple contains the value `#FIFA` in the `text` field or not. If the tuple contains `#FIFA` in the `text` field, then the method returns true. Otherwise, it returns false.

The `Print` class extends the `org.apache.storm.trident.operation.BaseFilter` class and contains the `isKeep(TridentTuple tuple)` method. The `isKeep()` method prints the input tuple and returns true.

4. Create a `TridentHelloWorldTopology` class in a
   `com.stormadvance.storm_trident` package. This class defines the hello
   world Trident topology:

```
public class TridentHelloWorldTopology {
    public static void main(String[] args) throws Exception {
            Config conf = new Config();
            conf.setMaxSpoutPending(20);
            if (args.length == 0) {
                    LocalCluster cluster = new LocalCluster();
                    cluster.submitTopology("Count", conf,
buildTopology());
            } else {
                    conf.setNumWorkers(3);
                    StormSubmitter.submitTopology(args[0], conf,
buildTopology());
            }
    }
    public static StormTopologybuildTopology() {

            FakeTweetSpout spout = new FakeTweetSpout(10);
            TridentTopology topology = new TridentTopology();

            topology.newStream("spout1", spout)
                    .shuffle()
                    .each(new Fields("text", "Country"),
                            new TridentUtility.TweetFilter())
                    .groupBy(new Fields("Country"))
                    .aggregate(new Fields("Country"), new Count(),
                            new Fields("count"))
                    .each(new Fields("count"), new
TridentUtility.Print())
                    .parallelismHint(2);

            return topology.build();
    }
}
```

Let's understand the code line by line. Firstly, we are creating an object of the
`TridentTopology` class for defining the Trident computation.

The `TridentTopology` contains a method called `newStream()`, which will take an input source as an argument. In this example, we are using `FakeTweetSpout` created in the non-transactional topology section as an input source. Like Storm, Trident also maintains the state of each input source in ZooKeeper. Here, the `FakeTweetSpout` string specifies the node in ZooKeeper where Trident maintains the metadata.

The spout emits a stream that has two fields, `text` and `Country`.

We are repartitioning the batch of tuples emitted by the input source using the `shuffle` operation. The next line of the topology definition applies `TweetFilter` on each tuple. `TweetFilter` filters out all those tuples that do not contain the `#FIFA` keyword.

The output of `TweetFilter` is grouped by the `Country` field. Then, we applied the `Count` aggregator to count the tweets for each country. Finally, we are applying a `Print` filter to print the output of the `aggregate` method.

Here is the console output of the `TridentHelloWorldTopology` class:

```
                                      ankit@impetus-1342.centos - TigerVNC
3141 [Thread-9] INFO  backtype.storm.daemon.executor - Loading executor spout0:[7 7]
3142 [Thread-9] INFO  backtype.storm.daemon.executor - Loaded executor tasks spout0:[7 7]
3143 [Thread-9] INFO  backtype.storm.daemon.executor - Finished loading executor spout0:[7 7]
3143 [Thread-26-spout0] INFO  backtype.storm.daemon.executor - Preparing bolt spout0:(7)
3144 [Thread-26-spout0] INFO  backtype.storm.daemon.executor - Prepared bolt spout0:(7)
3147 [Thread-9] INFO  backtype.storm.daemon.executor - Loading executor __system:[-1 -1]
3148 [Thread-9] INFO  backtype.storm.daemon.executor - Loaded executor tasks __system:[-1 -1]
3149 [Thread-9] INFO  backtype.storm.daemon.executor - Finished loading executor __system:[-1 -1]
3149 [Thread-28-__system] INFO  backtype.storm.daemon.executor - Preparing bolt __system:(-1)
3151 [Thread-28-__system] INFO  backtype.storm.daemon.executor - Prepared bolt __system:(-1)
3154 [Thread-9] INFO  backtype.storm.daemon.executor - Loading executor $mastercoord-bg0:[1 1]
3155 [Thread-9] INFO  backtype.storm.daemon.executor - Loaded executor tasks $mastercoord-bg0:[1 1]
3159 [Thread-9] INFO  backtype.storm.daemon.executor - Finished loading executor $mastercoord-bg0:[1 1]
3159 [Thread-30-$mastercoord-bg0] INFO  backtype.storm.daemon.executor - Opening spout $mastercoord-bg0:(1)
3160 [Thread-9] INFO  backtype.storm.daemon.worker - Launching receive-thread for b1bfbee5-be0d-4b1f-b436-ccc230d9ac9e:4
3161 [Thread-30-$mastercoord-bg0] INFO  com.netflix.curator.framework.imps.CuratorFrameworkImpl - Starting
3166 [Thread-9] INFO  backtype.storm.daemon.worker - Worker has topology config {"storm.id" "Count-1-1395506684", "dev.zookee
3167 [Thread-9] INFO  backtype.storm.daemon.worker - Worker b9fd29d4-e9c0-4e84-8026-6a7b22248e5e for storm Count-1-1395506684
3182 [Thread-30-$mastercoord-bg0] INFO  com.netflix.curator.framework.imps.CuratorFrameworkImpl - Starting
3192 [Thread-30-$mastercoord-bg0] INFO  backtype.storm.daemon.executor - Opened spout $mastercoord-bg0:(1)
3194 [Thread-30-$mastercoord-bg0] INFO  backtype.storm.daemon.executor - Activating spout $mastercoord-bg0:(1)
[2]
[1]
[1]
[1]
[2]
[2]
[2]
[4]
[1]
```

Here is a diagram that shows the execution of the hello world Trident topology:

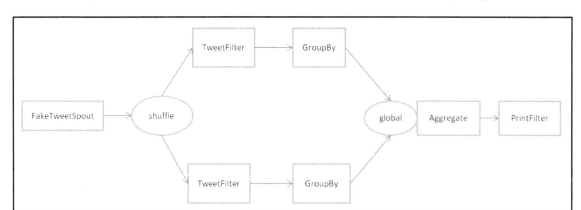

Trident state

Trident provides an abstraction for reading from and writing results to stateful sources. We can maintain the state either internally to the topology (memory), or we can store it in external sources (Memcached or Cassandra).

Let's consider that we are maintaining the output of the preceding hello world Trident topology in a database. Every time you process the tuple, the count of country present in a tuple is increased in the database. We can't achieve exactly-once processing by only maintaining a count in the database. The reason is that if any tuple failed during processing, then the failed tuple is retried. This gives us a problem while updating the state, because we are not sure whether the state of this tuple was updated previously or not. If the tuple has failed before updating the state, then retrying the tuple will increase the count in the database and make the state consistent. But if the tuple has failed after updating the state, then retrying the same tuple will again increase the count in the database and make the state inconsistent. Hence, by only maintaining a count in the database, we have no idea whether or not this tuple has been processed before. We need more details to take the right decision. We need to follow these steps to achieve the exactly-once processing semantics:

1. Process the tuples in small batches.
2. Assign a unique ID to each batch (transactional ID). If the batch is retried, it is given the same unique ID.
3. The state updates are ordered among batches. For example, the state update of batch 2 would not be possible until the state updates for batch 1 have completed.

If we create a topology by using the preceding three semantics, then we can easily take a decision whether the tuple is processed before or not.

Distributed RPC

Distributed RPC is used to query on and retrieve results from Trident topology on the fly. Storm has an in-built distributed RPC server. The distributed RPC server receives the RPC request from the client and passes it to the Storm topology. The topology processes the request and sends the result to the distributed RPC server, which is redirected by the distributed RPC server to the client.

We can configure the distributed RPC server by using the following properties in the `storm.yaml` file:

```
drpc.servers:
    - "nimbus-node"
```

Here, `nimbus-node` is the IP of the distributed RPC server.

Now, run this command on the `nimbus-node` machine to start the distributed RPC server:

> **bin/storm drpc**

Let's assume we are storing the count aggregation of hello world Trident topology in a database and want to retrieve the count for a given country on the fly. We would need to use the distributed RPC feature to achieve this. This example shows how we can incorporate the distributed RPC in the hello world Trident topology created in the previous section:

We are creating a `DistributedRPC` class that contains a `buildTopology()` method:

```
public class DistributedRPC {
  public static void main(String[] args) throws Exception {
    Config conf = new Config();
    conf.setMaxSpoutPending(20);
    LocalDRPCdrpc = new LocalDRPC();
    if (args.length == 0) {
      LocalCluster cluster = new LocalCluster();
      cluster.submitTopology("CountryCount", conf, buildTopology(drpc));
      Thread.sleep(2000);
      for(inti=0; i<100 ; i++) {
        System.out.println("Result - "+drpc.execute("Count", "Japan India
Europe"));
          Thread.sleep(1000);
```

```
      }
    } else {
      conf.setNumWorkers(3);
      StormSubmitter.submitTopology(args[0], conf, buildTopology(null));
      Thread.sleep(2000);
      DRPCClient client = new DRPCClient(conf, "RRPC-Server", 1234);
      System.out.println(client.execute("Count", "Japan India Europe"));
    }
  }

  public static StormTopologybuildTopology(LocalDRPCdrpc) {

    FakeTweetSpout spout = new FakeTweetSpout(10);
    TridentTopology topology = new TridentTopology();
    TridentStatecountryCount = topology.newStream("spout1", spout)
                    .shuffle()
                    .each(new Fields("text","Country"), new
TridentUtility.TweetFilter()).groupBy(new Fields("Country"))
                    .persistentAggregate(new MemoryMapState.Factory(),new
Fields("Country"), new Count(), new Fields("count"))
                    .parallelismHint(2);
    try {
      Thread.sleep(2000);
    } catch (InterruptedException e) {
    }
    topology.newDRPCStream("Count", drpc)
        .each(new Fields("args"), new TridentUtility.Split(), new
Fields("Country"))
        .stateQuery(countryCount, new Fields("Country"), new MapGet(),
                new Fields("count")).each(new Fields("count"),
                    new FilterNull());
    return topology.build();
  }
}
```

Let's understand the code line by line.

We are using `FakeTweetSpout` as an input source and the `TridentTopology` class to define the Trident computation.

In the next line, we are using the `persistentAggregate` function to represent the count aggregation of all the batches emitted. `MemoryMapState.Factory()` is used to maintain the count state. The `persistentAggregate` function knows how to store and update the aggregation in the source state:

```
persistentAggregate(new MemoryMapState.Factory(),new Fields("Country"), new
Count(), new Fields("count"))
```

The memory database stores the country name as a key and the aggregation count as a value, as shown here:

```
India 124
United State 145
Japan 130
Brazil 155
China 100
```

The `persistentAggregate` transforms the stream into a Trident `State` object. In this case, the Trident `State` object represents the count of each country so far.

The next part of the topology defines a distributed query to get the count of each country on the fly. The distributed RPC query takes as input a comma-separated list of countries and returns the count of the each country. Here is the piece of code that defines the distributed query portion:

```
topology.newDRPCStream("Count", drpc)
        .each(new Fields("args"), new TridentUtility.Split(), new
Fields("Country"))
        .stateQuery(countryCount, new Fields("Country"), new MapGet(),
                new Fields("count")).each(new Fields("count"),
                        new FilterNull());
```

The `Split` function is used to split the comma-separated list of countries. We have used a `stateQuery()` method to query the Trident `State` object that is defined in the first part of the topology. The `stateQuery()` takes in source of state--in this case, the countries count computed by the first part of the topology and a function for querying this function. We are using a `MapGet()` function, which gets the count for each country. Finally, the count of each country is returned as the query output.

Here is the piece of code that shows how we can pass input to a local distributed RPC:

```
System.out.println(drpc.execute("Count", "Japan,India,Europe"));
```

We have created an instance of `backtype.storm.LocalDRPC` to simulate the distributed RPC.

If you are running the distributed RPC server, then we need to create an instance of a distributed RPC client to execute the query. Here is the piece of code that shows how we can pass input to the distributed RPC server:

```
DRPCClient client = new DRPCClient(conf,"RRPC-Server", 1234);
System.out.println(client.execute("Count", "Japan,India,Europe"));
```

The Trident distributed RPC query executes like a normal RPC query, except these queries are run in parallel.

Here is the console output of the `DistributedRPC` class:

```
Console ☒
<terminated> DistributedRPC [Java Application] /usr/java/jdk1.6.0_31/bin/java (Mar 23, 2014 12:03:47 PM)
4543 [Thread-37-spout1] INFO  backtype.storm.daemon.executor - Opened spout spout1:(12)
4543 [Thread-37-spout1] INFO  backtype.storm.daemon.executor - Activating spout spout1:(12)
4547 [Thread-7] INFO  backtype.storm.daemon.executor - Loading executor __system:[-1 -1]
4547 [Thread-7] INFO  backtype.storm.daemon.executor - Loaded executor tasks __system:[-1 -1]
4548 [Thread-7] INFO  backtype.storm.daemon.executor - Finished loading executor __system:[-1 -1]
4548 [Thread-39-__system] INFO  backtype.storm.daemon.executor - Preparing bolt __system:(-1)
4550 [Thread-39-__system] INFO  backtype.storm.daemon.executor - Prepared bolt __system:(-1)
4553 [Thread-7] INFO  backtype.storm.daemon.executor - Loading executor $mastercoord-bg0:[1 1]
4554 [Thread-7] INFO  backtype.storm.daemon.executor - Loaded executor tasks $mastercoord-bg0:[1 1]
4555 [Thread-41-$mastercoord-bg0] INFO  backtype.storm.daemon.executor - Opening spout $mastercoord-bg0:(
4555 [Thread-7] INFO  backtype.storm.daemon.executor - Finished loading executor $mastercoord-bg0:[1 1]
4555 [Thread-7] INFO  backtype.storm.daemon.worker - Launching receive-thread for 99e01e9b-55fe-4917-b177
4555 [Thread-41-$mastercoord-bg0] INFO  com.netflix.curator.framework.imps.CuratorFrameworkImpl - Startin
4565 [Thread-7] INFO  backtype.storm.daemon.worker - Worker has topology config {"storm.id" "CountryCount
4566 [Thread-7] INFO  backtype.storm.daemon.worker - Worker 0011081f-ad41-40d7-af2b-f687e9fec7a9 for stor
4586 [Thread-41-$mastercoord-bg0] INFO  com.netflix.curator.framework.imps.CuratorFrameworkImpl - Startin
4596 [Thread-41-$mastercoord-bg0] INFO  backtype.storm.daemon.executor - Opened spout $mastercoord-bg0:(1
4596 [Thread-41-$mastercoord-bg0] INFO  backtype.storm.daemon.executor - Activating spout $mastercoord-bg
[["Japan,India,Europe","Japan",42]]
[["Japan,India,Europe","Japan",77]]
[["Japan,India,Europe","India",86]]
[["Japan,India,Europe","Japan",125]]
[["Japan,India,Europe","India",135]]
[["Japan,India,Europe","India",165]]
[["Japan,India,Europe","India",186]]
[["Japan,India,Europe","India",220]]
[["Japan,India,Europe","Japan",247]]
[["Japan,India,Europe","India",270]]
```

When to use Trident

It is very easy to achieve exactly-once processing using Trident topology and Trident meant for the same. On the other hand, it would be difficult to achieve the exactly-once processing in the case of vanilla Storm. Hence, Trident will be useful for that use case where we have require exactly-once processing.

Trident is not fit for all use cases, especially for high-performance use cases, because Trident adds complexity on Storm and manages the state.

Summary

In this chapter, we mainly concentrated on the Trident sample topology, the Trident `groupBy` operation, and the non-transactional topology. We also covered how we can query on the fly on a Trident topology using distributed RPC.

In the next chapter, we will cover the different types of Storm scheduler.

6
Storm Scheduler

In the previous chapters, we covered the basics of Storm, the installation of Storm, the development and deployment of Storm, and the Trident topology in Storm clusters. In this chapter, we are focusing on Storm schedulers.

In this chapter, we are going to cover the following points:

- Introduction to Storm schedulers
- Default scheduler
- Isolation scheduler
- Resource-aware scheduler
- Customer-aware scheduler

Introduction to Storm scheduler

As mentioned in the first two chapters, the Nimbus is responsible for deploying the topology and the supervisor is responsible for performing the computation tasks as defined in a Storm topology's spouts and bolts components. As we have shown, we can configure the number of worker slots for each supervisor node that are assigned to a topology as per the scheduler policy, as well as the number of workers allocated to a topology. In short, Storm schedulers help the Nimbus to decide the worker distribution of any given topology.

Default scheduler

The Storm default scheduler assigns component executors as evenly as possible between all the workers (supervisor slots) assigned to a given topology.

Let's consider a sample topology with one spout and one bolt, with both components having two executors. The following diagram shows the assignment of executors if we have submitted the topology by allocating two workers (supervisor slots):

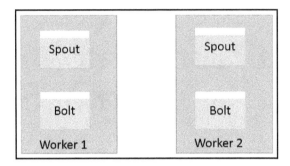

As shown in the preceding diagram, each worker node contains one executor for a spout and one executor for a bolt. The even distribution of executors between workers is only possible if the number of executors in each component is divisible by the number of workers assigned to a topology.

Isolation scheduler

The isolation scheduler provides a mechanism for the easy and safe sharing of Storm cluster resources among many topologies. The isolation scheduler helps to allocate/reserve the dedicated sets of Storm nodes for topologies within the Storm cluster.

We need to define the following property in the Nimbus configuration file to switch to the isolation scheduler:

```
storm.scheduler: org.apache.storm.scheduler.IsolationScheduler
```

We can allocate/reserve the resources for any topology by specifying the topology name and the number of nodes inside the isolation.scheduler.machines property, as mentioned in the following section. We need to define the isolation.scheduler.machines property in the Nimbus configuration, as Nimbus is responsible for the distribution of topology workers between Storm nodes:

```
isolation.scheduler.machines:
   "Topology-Test1": 2
   "Topology-Test2": 1
   "Topology-Test3": 4
```

In the preceding configuration, two nodes are assigned to `Topology-Test1`, one node is assigned to `Topology-Test2`, and four nodes are assigned to `Topology-Test3`.

Here are the key points of the isolation scheduler:

- The topologies mentioned in the isolation list are given priority over non-isolation topologies, which means that resources will be allocated to isolation topologies first if there's competition with non-isolation topologies
- There is no way to change the isolation setting of topologies during runtime
- The isolation topology solves the multitenancy problem by assigning dedicated machines to topologies

Resource-aware scheduler

A resource-aware scheduler helps users specify the amount of resources required for a single instance of any component (spout or bolt). We can enable the resource-aware scheduler by specifying the following property in the `storm.yaml` file:

```
storm.scheduler:
"org.apache.storm.scheduler.resource.ResourceAwareScheduler"
```

Component-level configuration

You can allocate the memory requirement to any component. Here are the methods available to allocate the memory to a single instance of any component:

```
public T setMemoryLoad(Number onHeap, Number offHeap)
```

Alternatively, you can use the following:

```
public T setMemoryLoad(Number onHeap)
```

The following is the definition of each argument:

- `onHeap`: The amount of on heap space an instance of this component will consume in megabytes
- `offHeap`: The amount of off heap space an instance of this component will consume in megabytes

The data type of both `onHeap` and `offHeap` is `Number`, and the default value is `0.0`.

Memory usage example

Let's consider a topology that has two components--one spout and one bolt:

```
SpoutDeclarer spout1 = builder.setSpout("spout1", new spoutComponent(), 4);
spout1.setMemoryLoad(1024.0, 512.0);
builder.setBolt("bolt1", new boltComponent(), 5).setMemoryLoad(512.0);
```

The memory request for a single instance of the `spout1` component is 1.5 GB (1 GB on heap and 0.5 GB off heap), which means that the total memory request for the `spout1` component is 4 x 1.5 GB = 6 GB.

The memory request for a single instance of the `bolt1` component is 0.5 GB (0.5 GB on heap and 0.0 GB off heap), which means that the total memory request for the `bolt1` component is 5 x 0.5 GB = 2.5 GB. The method of calculating the total memory required for both components can be summarized as follows:

Total memory allocated to topology = spout1 + bolt1 = 6 + 2.5 = 8.5 GB

You can also allocate the CPU requirement to any component.

Here is the method required to allocate the amount of CPU resources to a single instance of any component:

```
public T setCPULoad(Double amount)
```

The `amount` is the amount of CPU resources an instance of any given component will consume. CPU usage is a difficult concept to define. Different CPU architectures perform differently depending on the task at hand. By convention, a CPU core will typically have 100 points. If you feel that your processors are more or less powerful, you can adjust this accordingly. Heavy tasks that are CPU-bound will get 100 points, as they can consume an entire core. Medium tasks should get 50, light tasks 25, and tiny tasks 10.

CPU usage example

Let's consider a topology that has two components--one spout and one bolt:

```
SpoutDeclarer spout1 = builder.setSpout("spout1", new spoutComponent(), 4);
spout1.setCPULoad(15.0);
builder.setBolt("bolt1", new boltComponent(), 5).setCPULoad(450.0);
```

Worker-level configuration

You can allocate the heap size per worker/slot. Here is the method required to define the heap size of each worker node:

```
public void setTopologyWorkerMaxHeapSize(Number size)
```

Here, `size` is the amount of heap space available to a single worker in megabytes.

Here is an example:

```
Config conf = new Config();
conf.setTopologyWorkerMaxHeapSize(1024.0);
```

Node-level configuration

We can configure the amount of memory and CPU a Storm node can use by setting the following properties in the `storm.yaml` file. We need to set the following properties on each Storm node:

```
supervisor.memory.capacity.mb: [amount<Double>]
supervisor.cpu.capacity: [amount<Double>]
```

Here is an example:

```
supervisor.memory.capacity.mb: 10480.0
supervisor.cpu.capacity: 100.0
```

Here, `100` means an entire core, as discussed previously.

Global component configuration

As mentioned in the previous section, we can define the memory and CPU requirements for each component by defining the topology. The user can also set the default resource usage of components in the `storm.yaml` file. If we are defining the component configuration in the code, then the code value will overwrite the default one:

```
//default value if on heap memory requirement is not specified for a
component
topology.component.resources.onheap.memory.mb: 128.0

//default value if off heap memory requirement is not specified for a
component
topology.component.resources.offheap.memory.mb: 0.0
```

```
//default value if CPU requirement is not specified for a component
topology.component.cpu.pcore.percent: 10.0

//default value for the max heap size for a worker
topology.worker.max.heap.size.mb: 768.0
```

Custom scheduler

In Storm, Nimbus uses a scheduler to assign tasks to the supervisors. The default scheduler aims to allocate computing resources evenly to topologies. It works well in terms of fairness among topologies, but it is impossible for users to predict the placement of topology components in the Storm cluster, regarding which component of a topology needs to be assigned to which supervisor node.

Let's consider an example. Say that we have a topology that has one spout and two bolts, and each of the components has one executor and one task. The following diagram shows the distribution of the topology if we submit the topology to a Storm cluster. Assume that the number of workers assigned to the topology is three and the number of supervisors in the Storm cluster is three:

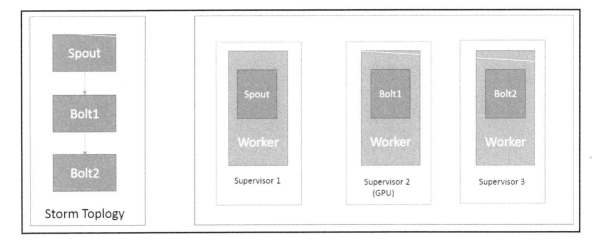

Let's assume that the last bolt in our topology, **Bolt2**, needs to process some data using a GPU rather than the CPU, and there's only one of the supervisors with a GPU. We need to write our own custom scheduler to achieve the assignment of any component to a specific supervisor node. Here are the steps we need to perform to achieve this:

1. Configure changes in the supervisor node.
2. Configure settings at the component level.
3. Write a custom scheduler class.
4. Register the customer scheduler class.

Configuration changes in the supervisor node

Storm offers a field in the supervisor's configuration for users to specify custom scheduling metadata. In this case, we type /tag in the supervisors, along with the type they are running on, which we do with a single line of config in their $STORM_HOME/conf/storm.yaml file. For example, each supervisor node should have the following in its config:

```
supervisor.scheduler.meta:
  type: GPU
```

We need to restart the supervisor node after adding the configuration changes to each supervisor node. You need to use the CPU type for all non-GPU machines.

Configuration setting at component level

This step is done when building the topology with TopologyBuilder in the main method of a topology. ComponentConfigurationDeclarer has a method called addConfiguration(String config, String value) that allows adding of custom configuration--that is, metadata. In our case, we add the type information using this method:

```
TopologyBuilder builder = new TopologyBuilder();
builder.setSpout("spout", new SampleSpout(), 1); builder.setBolt("bolt1",
new ExampleBolt1(), 1).shuffleGrouping("spout");
builder.setBolt("bolt3", new SampleBolt2(),
1).shuffleGrouping("bolt2").addConfiguration("type", "GPU");
```

The preceding code shows that we have typed our bolt2 component with type as GPU.

Writing a custom supervisor class

We can write our `CustomScheduler` class by implementing the
`org.apache.storm.scheduler.IScheduler` interface. The interface contains two
important methods:

- `prepare(Map conf)`: This method only initializes the scheduler
- `schedule(Topologies topologies, Cluster cluster)`: This method
  contains logic that is responsible for topology workers in the cluster supervisor
  slots

`CustomScheduler` contains the following private method, which is responsible for
assigning workers to the cluster supervisor slots.

The `getSupervisorsByType()` method returns the map. The key of the map represents
the node type (for example, CPU or GPU) and the value contains the list of supervisor
nodes of that type:

```
        private Map<String, ArrayList<SupervisorDetails>> getSupervisorsByType(
                Collection<SupervisorDetails> supervisorDetails
        ) {
            // A map of type -> supervisors, to help with scheduling of
    components with specific types
            Map<String, ArrayList<SupervisorDetails>> supervisorsByType = new
    HashMap<String, ArrayList<SupervisorDetails>>();

            for (SupervisorDetails supervisor : supervisorDetails) {
                @SuppressWarnings("unchecked")
                Map<String, String> metadata = (Map<String, String>)
    supervisor.getSchedulerMeta();

                String types;

                if (metadata == null) {
                    types = unType;
                } else {
                    types = metadata.get("types");

                    if (types == null) {
                        types = unType;
                    }
                }
```

```
                // If the supervisor has types attached to it, handle it by
        populating the supervisorsByType map.
                // Loop through each of the types to handle individually
                for (String type : types.split(",")) {
                    type = type.trim();

                    if (supervisorsByType.containsKey(type)) {
                        // If we've already seen this type, then just add the
        supervisor to the existing ArrayList.
                        supervisorsByType.get(type).add(supervisor);
                    } else {
                        // If this type is new, then create a new
        ArrayList<SupervisorDetails>,
                        // add the current supervisor, and populate the map's
        type entry with it.
                        ArrayList<SupervisorDetails> newSupervisorList = new
        ArrayList<SupervisorDetails>();
                        newSupervisorList.add(supervisor);
                        supervisorsByType.put(type, newSupervisorList);
                    }
                }
            }

            return supervisorsByType;
        }
```

The `populateComponentsByType()` method also returns the map. The key of the map represents the type (CPU or GPU) and the value contains the list of components of the topology that needs to be assigned to that type of supervisor node. We use an untyped type here to group components with no types. The purpose of this is to effectively handle these untyped components in the same way that the default scheduler performs its assigning. That means that a topology with no typed components will be successfully scheduled in the same way, with no issues, across untyped supervisors:

```
        private <T> void populateComponentsByType(
                Map<String, ArrayList<String>> componentsByType,
                Map<String, T> components
        ) {
            // Type T can be either Bolt or SpoutSpec, so that this logic can
        be reused for both component types
            JSONParser parser = new JSONParser();

            for (Entry<String, T> componentEntry : components.entrySet()) {
                JSONObject conf = null;

                String componentID = componentEntry.getKey();
                T component = componentEntry.getValue();
```

```
            try {
                // Get the component's conf irrespective of its type (via
java reflection)
                Method getCommonComponentMethod =
component.getClass().getMethod("get_common");
                ComponentCommon commonComponent = (ComponentCommon)
getCommonComponentMethod.invoke(component);
                conf = (JSONObject)
parser.parse(commonComponent.get_json_conf());
            } catch (Exception ex) {
                ex.printStackTrace();
            }

            String types;

            // If there's no config, use a fake type to group all untypeged
components
            if (conf == null) {
                types = unType;
            } else {
                types = (String) conf.get("types");

                // If there are no types, use a fake type to group all
untypeged components
                if (types == null) {
                    types = unType;
                }
            }

            // If the component has types attached to it, handle it by
populating the componentsByType map.
            // Loop through each of the types to handle individually
            for (String type : types.split(",")) {
                type = type.trim();

                if (componentsByType.containsKey(type)) {
                    // If we've already seen this type, then just add the
component to the existing ArrayList.
                    componentsByType.get(type).add(componentID);
                } else {
                    // If this type is new, then create a new ArrayList,
                    // add the current component, and populate the map's
type entry with it.
                    ArrayList<String> newComponentList = new
ArrayList<String>();
                    newComponentList.add(componentID);
                    componentsByType.put(type, newComponentList);
                }
```

```
                    }
               }
          }
```

The `populateComponentsByTypeWithStormInternals()` method returns the details of the internal components that Storm launches to a topology's data flow:

```
    private void populateComponentsByTypeWithStormInternals(
            Map<String, ArrayList<String>> componentsByType,
            Set<String> components
    ) {
        // Storm uses some internal components, like __acker.
        // These components are topology-agnostic and are therefore not
accessible through a StormTopology object.
        // While a bit hacky, this is a way to make sure that we schedule
those components along with our topology ones:
        // we treat these internal components as regular untypeged
components and add them to the componentsByType map.

        for (String componentID : components) {
            if (componentID.startsWith("__")) {
                if (componentsByType.containsKey(unType)) {
                    // If we've already seen untypeged components, then
just add the component to the existing ArrayList.
                    componentsByType.get(unType).add(componentID);
                } else {
                    // If this is the first untypeged component we see,
then create a new ArrayList,
                    // add the current component, and populate the map's
untypeged entry with it.
                    ArrayList<String> newComponentList = new
ArrayList<String>();
                    newComponentList.add(componentID);
                    componentsByType.put(unType, newComponentList);
                }
            }
        }
    }
```

The first three methods manage the maps of the supervisors and components. Now, we will write the `typeAwareScheduler()` method, which will use both the maps:

```
    private void typeAwareSchedule(Topologies topologies, Cluster cluster)
    {
        Collection<SupervisorDetails> supervisorDetails =
cluster.getSupervisors().values();

        // Get the lists of typed and unreserved supervisors.
```

```
        Map<String, ArrayList<SupervisorDetails>> supervisorsByType =
getSupervisorsByType(supervisorDetails);

        for (TopologyDetails topologyDetails :
cluster.needsSchedulingTopologies(topologies)) {
            StormTopology stormTopology = topologyDetails.getTopology();
            String topologyID = topologyDetails.getId();

            // Get components from topology
            Map<String, Bolt> bolts = stormTopology.get_bolts();
            Map<String, SpoutSpec> spouts = stormTopology.get_spouts();

            // Get a map of component to executors
            Map<String, List<ExecutorDetails>> executorsByComponent =
cluster.getNeedsSchedulingComponentToExecutors(
                    topologyDetails
            );

            // Get a map of type to components
            Map<String, ArrayList<String>> componentsByType = new
HashMap<String, ArrayList<String>>();
            populateComponentsByType(componentsByType, bolts);
            populateComponentsByType(componentsByType, spouts);
            populateComponentsByTypeWithStormInternals(componentsByType,
executorsByComponent.keySet());

            // Get a map of type to executors
            Map<String, ArrayList<ExecutorDetails>>
executorsToBeScheduledByType = getExecutorsToBeScheduledByType(
                    cluster, topologyDetails, componentsByType
            );

            // Initialise a map of slot -> executors
            Map<WorkerSlot, ArrayList<ExecutorDetails>>
componentExecutorsToSlotsMap = (
                    new HashMap<WorkerSlot, ArrayList<ExecutorDetails>>()
            );

            // Time to match everything up!
            for (Entry<String, ArrayList<ExecutorDetails>> entry :
executorsToBeScheduledByType.entrySet()) {
                String type = entry.getKey();

                ArrayList<ExecutorDetails> executorsForType =
entry.getValue();
                ArrayList<SupervisorDetails> supervisorsForType =
supervisorsByType.get(type);
                ArrayList<String> componentsForType =
```

```
componentsByType.get(type);

                try {
                    populateComponentExecutorsToSlotsMap(
                            componentExecutorsToSlotsMap,
                            cluster, topologyDetails, supervisorsForType,
executorsForType, componentsForType, type
                    );
                } catch (Exception e) {
                    e.printStackTrace();

                    // Cut this scheduling short to avoid partial
scheduling.
                    return;
                }
            }

            // Do the actual assigning
            // We do this as a separate step to only perform any assigning
if there have been no issues so far.
            // That's aimed at avoiding partial scheduling from occurring,
with some components already scheduled
            // and alive, while others cannot be scheduled.
            for (Entry<WorkerSlot, ArrayList<ExecutorDetails>> entry :
componentExecutorsToSlotsMap.entrySet()) {
                WorkerSlot slotToAssign = entry.getKey();
                ArrayList<ExecutorDetails> executorsToAssign =
entry.getValue();

                cluster.assign(slotToAssign, topologyID,
executorsToAssign);
            }

            // If we've reached this far, then scheduling must have been
successful
            cluster.setStatus(topologyID, "SCHEDULING SUCCESSFUL");
        }
    }
```

Apart from the preceding four methods, we are also using more methods that do the following things.

Converting component IDs to executors

Now let's make the jump from component IDs to actual executors, as that's the level at which the Storm cluster deals with assignments.

The process is quite straightforward:

- Get a map of executors by component from the cluster
- Check which components' executors need scheduling, according to the cluster
- Create a map of the types to the executors, populating only those executors that are awaiting scheduling:

```
private Set<ExecutorDetails> getAllAliveExecutors(Cluster cluster,
TopologyDetails topologyDetails) {
        // Get the existing assignment of the current topology as it's live
in the cluster
        SchedulerAssignment existingAssignment =
cluster.getAssignmentById(topologyDetails.getId());

        // Return alive executors, if any, otherwise an empty set
        if (existingAssignment != null) {
            return existingAssignment.getExecutors();
        } else {
            return new HashSet<ExecutorDetails>();
        }
    }

    private Map<String, ArrayList<ExecutorDetails>>
getExecutorsToBeScheduledByType(
            Cluster cluster,
            TopologyDetails topologyDetails,
            Map<String, ArrayList<String>> componentsPerType
    ) {
        // Initialise the return value
        Map<String, ArrayList<ExecutorDetails>> executorsByType = new
HashMap<String, ArrayList<ExecutorDetails>>();

        // Find which topology executors are already assigned
        Set<ExecutorDetails> aliveExecutors = getAllAliveExecutors(cluster,
topologyDetails);

        // Get a map of component to executors for the topology that need
scheduling
        Map<String, List<ExecutorDetails>> executorsByComponent =
cluster.getNeedsSchedulingComponentToExecutors(
                topologyDetails
```

```
        );

        // Loop through componentsPerType to populate the map
        for (Entry<String, ArrayList<String>> entry :
componentsPerType.entrySet()) {
            String type = entry.getKey();
            ArrayList<String> componentIDs = entry.getValue();

            // Initialise the map entry for the current type
            ArrayList<ExecutorDetails> executorsForType = new
ArrayList<ExecutorDetails>();

            // Loop through this type's component IDs
            for (String componentID : componentIDs) {
                // Fetch the executors for the current component ID
                List<ExecutorDetails> executorsForComponent =
executorsByComponent.get(componentID);

                if (executorsForComponent == null) {
                    continue;
                }

                // Convert the list of executors to a set
                Set<ExecutorDetails> executorsToAssignForComponent = new
HashSet<ExecutorDetails>(
                        executorsForComponent
                );

                // Remove already assigned executors from the set of
executors to assign, if any
                executorsToAssignForComponent.removeAll(aliveExecutors);

                // Add the component's waiting to be assigned executors to
the current type executors
                executorsForType.addAll(executorsToAssignForComponent);
            }

            // Populate the map of executors by type after looping through
all of the type's components,
            // if there are any executors to be scheduled
            if (!executorsForType.isEmpty()) {
                executorsByType.put(type, executorsForType);
            }
        }

        return executorsByType;
}
```

Converting supervisors to slots

And now for the final conversion we have to perform: jumping from supervisors down to slots. As before with components and their executors, we need this because the cluster assigns executors at the slot level, not the supervisor level.

There are a few things to do at this point; we have broken the process down into smaller methods to preserve readability. The main steps we need to perform are as follows:

Find out which slots we can assign to, given a list of supervisors for a type. This is simply the case of using a for loop that collects all supervisors' slots, and then returning as many of the slots as are requested by the topology.

Divide the executors awaiting scheduling for the type into even groups across the slots.

Populate a map with entries in the slot to the executors.

The idea here is to call the `populateComponentExecutorsToSlotsMap` method once per type, which results in a single map holding all the assignments we need to perform.

As explained in the code's comments, we previously found that sometimes we would eagerly assign a type's executors to a slot, only to have a successive type fail to assign its executors, leading to partial scheduling. We have since made sure that the flow of scheduling ensures that no partial scheduling is ever performed (either all are scheduled or none are), at the cost of an extra for loop, as we believe that's a cleaner state for a topology to be in:

```
    private void handleFailedScheduling(
            Cluster cluster,
            TopologyDetails topologyDetails,
            String message
    ) throws Exception {
        // This is the prefix of the message displayed on Storm's UI for
any unsuccessful scheduling
        String unsuccessfulSchedulingMessage = "SCHEDULING FAILED: ";

        cluster.setStatus(topologyDetails.getId(),
unsuccessfulSchedulingMessage + message);
        throw new Exception(message);
    }

    private Set<WorkerSlot> getAllAliveSlots(Cluster cluster,
TopologyDetails topologyDetails) {
        // Get the existing assignment of the current topology as it's live
in the cluster
        SchedulerAssignment existingAssignment =
```

```
cluster.getAssignmentById(topologyDetails.getId());

        // Return alive slots, if any, otherwise an empty set
        if (existingAssignment != null) {
            return existingAssignment.getSlots();
        } else {
            return new HashSet<WorkerSlot>();
        }
    }

    private List<WorkerSlot> getAllSlotsToAssign(
            Cluster cluster,
            TopologyDetails topologyDetails,
            List<SupervisorDetails> supervisors,
            List<String> componentsForType,
            String type
    ) throws Exception {
        String topologyID = topologyDetails.getId();

        // Collect the available slots of each of the supervisors we were
given in a list
        List<WorkerSlot> availableSlots = new ArrayList<WorkerSlot>();
        for (SupervisorDetails supervisor : supervisors) {
            availableSlots.addAll(cluster.getAvailableSlots(supervisor));
        }

        if (availableSlots.isEmpty()) {
            // This is bad, we have supervisors and executors to assign,
but no available slots!
            String message = String.format(
                    "No slots are available for assigning executors for
type %s (components: %s)",
                    type, componentsForType
            );
            handleFailedScheduling(cluster, topologyDetails, message);
        }

        Set<WorkerSlot> aliveSlots = getAllAliveSlots(cluster,
topologyDetails);

        int numAvailableSlots = availableSlots.size();
        int numSlotsNeeded = topologyDetails.getNumWorkers() -
aliveSlots.size();

        // We want to check that we have enough available slots
        // based on the topology's number of workers and already assigned
slots.
        if (numAvailableSlots < numSlotsNeeded) {
```

```
                // This is bad, we don't have enough slots to assign to!
                String message = String.format(
                        "Not enough slots available for assigning executors for
type %s (components: %s). "
                                + "Need %s slots to schedule but found only
%s",
                        type, componentsForType, numSlotsNeeded,
numAvailableSlots
                );
                handleFailedScheduling(cluster, topologyDetails, message);
            }

        // Now we can use only as many slots as are required.
        return availableSlots.subList(0, numSlotsNeeded);
    }

    private Map<WorkerSlot, ArrayList<ExecutorDetails>>
getAllExecutorsBySlot(
            List<WorkerSlot> slots,
            List<ExecutorDetails> executors
    ) {
        Map<WorkerSlot, ArrayList<ExecutorDetails>> assignments = new
HashMap<WorkerSlot, ArrayList<ExecutorDetails>>();

        int numberOfSlots = slots.size();

        // We want to split the executors as evenly as possible, across
each slot available,
        // so we assign each executor to a slot via round robin
        for (int i = 0; i < executors.size(); i++) {
            WorkerSlot slotToAssign = slots.get(i % numberOfSlots);
            ExecutorDetails executorToAssign = executors.get(i);

            if (assignments.containsKey(slotToAssign)) {
                // If we've already seen this slot, then just add the
executor to the existing ArrayList.
                assignments.get(slotToAssign).add(executorToAssign);
            } else {
                // If this slot is new, then create a new ArrayList,
                // add the current executor, and populate the map's slot
entry with it.
                ArrayList<ExecutorDetails> newExecutorList = new
ArrayList<ExecutorDetails>();
                newExecutorList.add(executorToAssign);
                assignments.put(slotToAssign, newExecutorList);
            }
        }
```

```
            return assignments;
    }

    private void populateComponentExecutorsToSlotsMap(
            Map<WorkerSlot, ArrayList<ExecutorDetails>>
componentExecutorsToSlotsMap,
            Cluster cluster,
            TopologyDetails topologyDetails,
            List<SupervisorDetails> supervisors,
            List<ExecutorDetails> executors,
            List<String> componentsForType,
            String type
    ) throws Exception {
        String topologyID = topologyDetails.getId();

        if (supervisors == null) {
            // This is bad, we don't have any supervisors but have
executors to assign!
            String message = String.format(
                    "No supervisors given for executors %s of topology %s
and type %s (components: %s)",
                    executors, topologyID, type, componentsForType
            );
            handleFailedScheduling(cluster, topologyDetails, message);
        }

        List<WorkerSlot> slotsToAssign = getAllSlotsToAssign(
                cluster, topologyDetails, supervisors, componentsForType,
type
        );

        // Divide the executors evenly across the slots and get a map of
slot to executors
        Map<WorkerSlot, ArrayList<ExecutorDetails>> executorsBySlot =
getAllExecutorsBySlot(
                slotsToAssign, executors
        );

        for (Entry<WorkerSlot, ArrayList<ExecutorDetails>> entry :
executorsBySlot.entrySet()) {
            WorkerSlot slotToAssign = entry.getKey();
            ArrayList<ExecutorDetails> executorsToAssign =
entry.getValue();

            // Assign the topology's executors to slots in the cluster's
supervisors
            componentExecutorsToSlotsMap.put(slotToAssign,
executorsToAssign);
```

```
        }
    }
```

Registering a CustomScheduler class

We need to create a JAR for the `CustomScheduler` class, and place it in `$STORM_HOME/lib/`, and tell Nimbus to use the new scheduler by appending the following lines to the configuration file at `$STORM_HOME/conf/storm.yaml`:

```
storm.scheduler: "com.stormadvance.storm_kafka_topology.CustomScheduler"
```

Restart the Nimbus daemon to reflect the changes to the configuration.

Now, if we deploy the same topology shown in the previous diagram, then the distribution of executors will look like this (**Bolt2** is assigned to a GPU-typed supervisor):

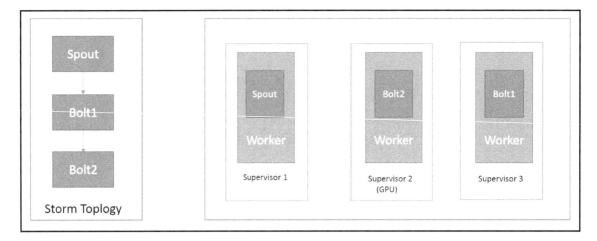

Summary

In this chapter, we learned about the built-in Storm scheduler and also covered how we can write and configure a custom scheduler.

In the next chapter, we will be covering the monitoring of a Storm cluster using Graphite and Ganglia.

7
Monitoring of Storm Cluster

In the previous chapters, we learned how we can deploy topologies on remote Storm clusters, how we can configure the parallelism of a topology, the different types of stream grouping, and so on. In this chapter, we will focus on how we can monitor and collect the statistics of topologies running on Storm clusters.

In this chapter, we will be covering the following topics:

- Collecting Storm metrics through the Nimbus thrift port
- Integration of Storm with Ganglia
- Installation of Graphite

Cluster statistics using the Nimbus thrift client

This section covers how we can collect cluster details (similar to the details shown on the Storm UI page) using the Nimbus thrift client. Extracting/collecting information through the Nimbus thrift client allows us to visualize the data.

The Nimbus thrift API is very rich, and exposes all the necessary information required to monitor the Storm cluster.

Fetching information with Nimbus thrift

In this section, we will be creating a Java project that will contain classes that will perform the following operations using the Nimbus thrift client:

- Collect the Nimbus configuration
- Collect the supervisor statistics
- Collect the topology statistics
- Collect the spout statistics for a given topology
- Collect the bolt statistics for a given topology
- Kill the given topology

The following are the steps to fetch the cluster details using the Nimbus thrift client:

1. Create a Maven project by using `com.stormadvance` as `groupId` and `stormmonitoring` as `artifactId`.

2. Add the following dependencies to the `pom.xml` file:

```
<dependency>
  <groupId>org.apache.storm</groupId>
  <artifactId>storm-core</artifactId>
  <version>1.0.2</version>
  <scope>provided</scope>
</dependency>
```

3. Create a utility class, `ThriftClient`, in the `com.stormadvance` package. The `ThriftClient` class contains logic to make a connection with the Nimbus thrift server and return the Nimbus client:

```
public class ThriftClient {
  // IP of the Storm UI node
  private static final String STORM_UI_NODE = "127.0.0.1";
  public Client getClient() {
    // Set the IP and port of thrift server.
    // By default, the thrift server start on port 6627
    TSocket socket = new TSocket(STORM_UI_NODE, 6627);
    TFramedTransport tFramedTransport = new
TFramedTransport(socket);
    TBinaryProtocol tBinaryProtocol = new
TBinaryProtocol(tFramedTransport);
    Client client = new Client(tBinaryProtocol);
    try {
      // Open the connection with thrift client.
      tFramedTransport.open();
```

```
       }catch(Exception exception) {
          throw new RuntimeException("Error occurs while making
    connection with Nimbus thrift server");
        }
        // return the Nimbus Thrift client.
        return client;
      }
    }
```

4. Let's create a class, `NimbusConfiguration`, in the `com.stormadvance` package.
   This class contains logic to collect the Nimbus configuration using the Nimbus
   client:

```
    public class NimbusConfiguration {
      public void printNimbusStats() {
        try {
          ThriftClient thriftClient = new ThriftClient();
          Client client = thriftClient.getClient();
          String nimbusConiguration = client.getNimbusConf();
          System.out.println("*************************************");
          System.out.println("Nimbus Configuration :
    "+nimbusConiguration);
          System.out.println("*************************************");
        }catch(Exception exception) {
          throw new RuntimeException("Error occure while fetching the
    Nimbus statistics : ");
        }
      }

      public static void main(String[] args) {
        new NimbusConfiguration().printNimbusStats();
      }
    }
```

   The preceding code uses the `getNimbusConf()` method of the class
   `org.apache.storm.generated.Nimbus.Client` to fetch the Nimbus
   configuration.

5. Create a class, `SupervisorStatistics`, in the `com.stormadvance` package to
   collect the information of all the supervisor nodes running in the Storm cluster:

```
    public class SupervisorStatistics {
      public void printSupervisorStatistics()  {
        try {
          ThriftClient thriftClient = new ThriftClient();
          Client client = thriftClient.getClient();
          // Get the cluster information.
```

```
      ClusterSummary clusterSummary = client.getClusterInfo();
      // Get the SupervisorSummary iterator
      Iterator<SupervisorSummary> supervisorsIterator =
clusterSummary.get_supervisors_iterator();
      while (supervisorsIterator.hasNext()) {
        // Print the information of supervisor node
        SupervisorSummary supervisorSummary = (SupervisorSummary)
supervisorsIterator.next();
System.out.println("*************************************");
        System.out.println("Supervisor Host IP :
"+supervisorSummary.get_host());
        System.out.println("Number of used workers :
"+supervisorSummary.get_num_used_workers());
        System.out.println("Number of workers :
"+supervisorSummary.get_num_workers());
        System.out.println("Supervisor ID :
"+supervisorSummary.get_supervisor_id());
        System.out.println("Supervisor uptime in seconds :
"+supervisorSummary.get_uptime_secs());

System.out.println("*************************************");
      }
    }catch (Exception e) {
      throw new RuntimeException("Error occure while getting
cluster info : ");
    }
  }

}
```

The `SupervisorStatistics` class uses the `getClusterInfo()` method of the `org.apache.storm.generated.Nimbus.Client` class to collect the cluster summary and then calls the `get_supervisors_iterator()` method of the `org.apache.storm.generated.ClusterSummary` class to get an iterator over the `org.apache.storm.generated.SupervisorSummary` class.

See the following for the output of the `SupervisorStatistics` class:

```
************************************
Supervisor Host IP : supervisor-1
Number of used workers : 1
Number of workers : 4
Supervisor ID : 872a45ce-5f58-466c-ba57-a29799991358
Supervisor uptime in seconds : 491
************************************
************************************
Supervisor Host IP : supervisor-2
Number of used workers : 2
Number of workers : 4
Supervisor ID : 5400bc2e-7e74-47af-a3b8-246705c4f1e7
Supervisor uptime in seconds : 475
************************************
```

6. Create a class `TopologyStatistics` in the `com.stormadvance` package to collect the information of all the topologies running in the Storm cluster:

```java
public class TopologyStatistics {

  public void printTopologyStatistics() {
    try {
      ThriftClient thriftClient = new ThriftClient();
      // Get the thrift client
      Client client = thriftClient.getClient();
      // Get the cluster info
      ClusterSummary clusterSummary = client.getClusterInfo();
      // Get the iterator over TopologySummary class
      Iterator<TopologySummary> topologiesIterator =
clusterSummary.get_topologies_iterator();
      while (topologiesIterator.hasNext()) {
        TopologySummary topologySummary =
topologiesIterator.next();
System.out.println("************************************");
        System.out.println("ID of topology: " +
topologySummary.get_id());
        System.out.println("Name of topology: " +
topologySummary.get_name());
        System.out.println("Number of Executors: " +
topologySummary.get_num_executors());
        System.out.println("Number of Tasks: " +
topologySummary.get_num_tasks());
```

```
         System.out.println("Number of Workers: " +
   topologySummary.get_num_workers());
         System.out.println("Status of toplogy: " +
   topologySummary.get_status());
         System.out.println("Topology uptime in seconds: " +
   topologySummary.get_uptime_secs());

   System.out.println("**************************************");
       }
     }catch (Exception exception) {
       throw new RuntimeException("Error occure while fetching the
   topolgies  information");
     }
   }
 }
```

The `TopologyStatistics` class uses the `get_topologies_iterator()` method of the `org.apache.storm.generated.ClusterSummary` class to get an iterator over class `org.apache.storm.generated.TopologySummary`. The class `TopologyStatistics` will print the value of the number of executors, the number of tasks, and the number of worker processes assigned to each topology.

7. Create a class `SpoutStatistics` in the `com.stormadvance` package to get the statistics of the spouts. The class `SpoutStatistics` contains a method `printSpoutStatistics(String topologyId)` to print the details of all the spouts served by a given topology:

```
   public class SpoutStatistics {

     private static final String DEFAULT = "default";
     private static final String ALL_TIME = ":all-time";

     public void printSpoutStatistics(String topologyId) {
       try {
         ThriftClient thriftClient = new ThriftClient();
         // Get the nimbus thrift client
         Client client = thriftClient.getClient();
         // Get the information of given topology
         TopologyInfo topologyInfo =
   client.getTopologyInfo(topologyId);
         Iterator<ExecutorSummary> executorSummaryIterator =
   topologyInfo.get_executors_iterator();
         while (executorSummaryIterator.hasNext()) {
           ExecutorSummary executorSummary =
   executorSummaryIterator.next();
           ExecutorStats executorStats = executorSummary.get_stats();
```

```
        if(executorStats !=null) {
           ExecutorSpecificStats executorSpecificStats =
executorStats.get_specific();
           String componentId = executorSummary.get_component_id();
           //
           if (executorSpecificStats.is_set_spout()) {
              SpoutStats spoutStats =
executorSpecificStats.get_spout();

System.out.println("*************************************");
              System.out.println("Component ID of Spout:- " +
componentId);
              System.out.println("Transferred:- " +
getAllTimeStat(executorStats.get_transferred(),ALL_TIME));
              System.out.println("Total tuples emitted:- " +
getAllTimeStat(executorStats.get_emitted(), ALL_TIME));
              System.out.println("Acked: " +
getAllTimeStat(spoutStats.get_acked(), ALL_TIME));
              System.out.println("Failed: " +
getAllTimeStat(spoutStats.get_failed(), ALL_TIME));
System.out.println("*************************************");
           }
         }
       }
    }catch (Exception exception) {
       throw new RuntimeException("Error occure while fetching the
spout information : "+exception);
    }
  }

  private static Long getAllTimeStat(Map<String, Map<String, Long>>
map, String statName) {
    if (map != null) {
      Long statValue = null;
      Map<String, Long> tempMap = map.get(statName);
      statValue = tempMap.get(DEFAULT);
      return statValue;
    }
    return 0L;
  }
  public static void main(String[] args) {
    new
SpoutStatistics().printSpoutStatistics("StormClusterTopology-1-1393
847956");
  }
}
```

The preceding class uses the `getTopologyInfo(topologyId)` method of the class `org.apache.storm.generated.Nimbus.Client` to fetch the information of a given topology. The `SpoutStatistics` class prints the following statistics of the spout:

- Spout ID
- Number of tuples emitted
- Number of tuples failed
- Number of tuples acknowledged

8. Create a class `BoltStatistics` in the `com.stormadvance` package to get the statistics of the bolts. The class `BoltStatistics` contains a method `printBoltStatistics(String topologyId)` to print the information of all the bolts served by a given topology:

```
public class BoltStatistics {

    private static final String DEFAULT = "default";
    private static final String ALL_TIME = ":all-time";

    public void printBoltStatistics(String topologyId) {

      try {
        ThriftClient thriftClient = new ThriftClient();
        // Get the Nimbus thrift server client
        Client client = thriftClient.getClient();
        // Get the information of given topology
        TopologyInfo topologyInfo =
client.getTopologyInfo(topologyId);
        Iterator<ExecutorSummary> executorSummaryIterator =
topologyInfo.get_executors_iterator();
        while (executorSummaryIterator.hasNext()) {
          // get the executor
          ExecutorSummary executorSummary =
executorSummaryIterator.next();
          ExecutorStats executorStats = executorSummary.get_stats();
          if (executorStats != null) {
            ExecutorSpecificStats executorSpecificStats =
executorStats.get_specific();
            String componentId = executorSummary.get_component_id();
            if (executorSpecificStats.is_set_bolt()) {
              BoltStats boltStats = executorSpecificStats.get_bolt();

System.out.println("************************************");
              System.out.println("Component ID of Bolt " +
```

```
componentId);
            System.out.println("Transferred: " +
getAllTimeStat(executorStats.get_transferred(), ALL_TIME));
            System.out.println("Emitted: " +
getAllTimeStat(executorStats.get_emitted(), ALL_TIME));
            System.out.println("Acked: " +
getBoltStats(boltStats.get_acked(), ALL_TIME));
            System.out.println("Failed: " +
getBoltStats(boltStats.get_failed(), ALL_TIME));
            System.out.println("Executed : " +
getBoltStats(boltStats.get_executed(), ALL_TIME));
System.out.println("***************************************");
          }
        }
      }
    } catch (Exception exception) {
      throw new RuntimeException("Error occure while fetching the
bolt information :"+exception);
    }
  }

  private static Long getAllTimeStat(Map<String, Map<String, Long>>
map, String statName) {
    if (map != null) {
      Long statValue = null;
      Map<String, Long> tempMap = map.get(statName);
      statValue = tempMap.get(DEFAULT);
      return statValue;
    }
    return 0L;
  }

  public static Long getBoltStats(Map<String, Map<GlobalStreamId,
Long>> map, String statName) {
    if (map != null) {
      Long statValue = null;
      Map<GlobalStreamId, Long> tempMap = map.get(statName);
      Set<GlobalStreamId> key = tempMap.keySet();
      if (key.size() > 0) {
        Iterator<GlobalStreamId> iterator = key.iterator();
        statValue = tempMap.get(iterator.next());
      }
      return statValue;
    }
    return 0L;
  }
```

```
      public static void main(String[] args) { new
    BoltStatistics().printBoltStatistics("StormClusterTopology-1-139384
    7956");
    }
```

The preceding class uses the `getTopologyInfo(topologyId)` method of the class `backtype.storm.generated.Nimbus.Client` to fetch the information of a given topology. The class `BoltStatistics` prints the following statistics of bolt:

- Bolt ID
- Number of tuples emitted
- Number of tuples failed
- Number of tuples acknowledged

9. Create a class `killTopology` in `com.stormadvance` package and define a method `kill` as mentioned as follows:

```
public void kill(String topologyId) {
  try {
    ThriftClient thriftClient = new ThriftClient();
    // Get the Nimbus thrift client
    Client client = thriftClient.getClient();
    // kill the given topology
    client.killTopology(topologyId);
  }catch (Exception exception) {
    throw new RuntimeException("Error occure while fetching the
spout information : "+exception);
  }
}
public static void main(String[] args) {
  new killTopology().kill("topologyId");
}
```

The preceding class uses the `killTopology(topologyId)` method of the class `org.apache.storm.generated.Nimbus.Client` to kill the topology.

In this section, we covered several methods of collecting the Storm cluster metrics/details using the Nimbus thrift client.

Monitoring the Storm cluster using JMX

This section will explain how we can monitor the Storm cluster using **Java Management Extensions** (**JMX**). The JMX is a set of specifications used to manage and monitor applications running in the JVM. We can collect or display Storm metrics, such as heap size, non-heap size, number of threads, number of loaded classes, heap and non-heap memory, virtual machine arguments, and managed objects on the JMX console. The following are the steps we need to perform to monitor the Storm cluster using JMX:

1. We will need to add the following line in the `storm.yaml` file of each supervisor node to enable JMX on each of them:

   ```
   supervisor.childopts: -verbose:gc -XX:+PrintGCTimeStamps -
   XX:+PrintGCDetails -Dcom.sun.management.jmxremote -
   Dcom.sun.management.jmxremote.ssl=false -
   Dcom.sun.management.jmxremote.authenticate=false -
   Dcom.sun.management.jmxremote.port=12346
   ```

   Here, `12346` is the port number used to collect the supervisor JVM metrics through JMX.

2. Add the following line in the `storm.yaml` file of the Nimbus machine to enable JMX on the Nimbus node:

   ```
   nimbus.childopts: -verbose:gc -XX:+PrintGCTimeStamps -
   XX:+PrintGCDetails -Dcom.sun.management.jmxremote -
   Dcom.sun.management.jmxremote.ssl=false -
   Dcom.sun.management.jmxremote.authenticate=false -
   Dcom.sun.management.jmxremote.port=12345
   ```

   Here, `12345` is the port number used to collect the Nimbus JVM metrics through JMX.

3. Also, you can collect the JVM metrics of worker processes by adding the following line in the `storm.yaml` file of each supervisor node:

   ```
   worker.childopts: -verbose:gc -XX:+PrintGCTimeStamps -
   XX:+PrintGCDetails -Dcom.sun.management.jmxremote -
   Dcom.sun.management.jmxremote.ssl=false -
   Dcom.sun.management.jmxremote.authenticate=false -
   Dcom.sun.management.jmxremote.port=2%ID%
   ```

Here, `%ID%` denotes the port number of the worker processes. If the port of the worker process is `6700`, then its JVM metrics are published on port number `26700` (`2%ID%`).

4. Now, run the following commands on any machine where Java is installed to start the JConsole:

```
cd $JAVA_HOME
./bin/jconsole
```

The following screenshot shows how we can connect to the supervisor JMX port using the JConsole:

If you open the JMX console on a machine other than the supervisor machine, then you need to use the IP address of the supervisor machine in the preceding screenshot instead of `127.0.0.1`.

Now, click on the **Connect** button to view the metrics of the supervisor node. The following screenshot shows what the metrics of the Storm supervisor node look like on the JMX console:

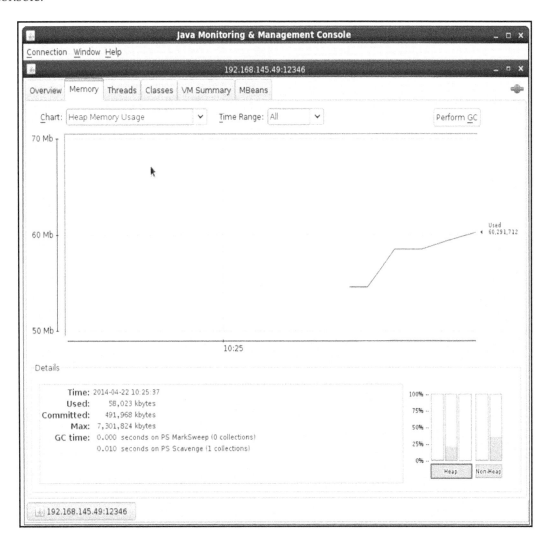

Similarly, you can collect the JVM metrics of the Nimbus node by specifying the IP address and the JMX port of the Nimbus machine on the JMX console.

The following section will explain how you can display the Storm cluster metrics on Ganglia.

Monitoring the Storm cluster using Ganglia

Ganglia is a monitoring tool that is used to collect the metrics of different types of processes that run on a cluster. In most applications, Ganglia is used as the centralized monitoring tool to display the metrics of all the processes that run on a cluster. Hence, it is essential that you enable the monitoring of the Storm cluster through Ganglia.

Ganglia has three important components:

- **Gmond**: This is a monitoring daemon of Ganglia that collects the metrics of nodes and sends this information to the Gmetad server. To collect the metrics of each Storm node, you will need to install the Gmond daemon on each of them.
- **Gmetad**: This gathers the metrics from all the Gmond nodes and stores them in the round-robin database.
- **Ganglia web interface**: This displays the metrics information in a graphical form.

Storm doesn't have built-in support to monitor the Storm cluster using Ganglia. However, with JMXTrans, you can enable Storm monitoring using Ganglia. The JMXTrans tool allows you to connect to any JVM, and fetches its JVM metrics without writing a single line of code. The JVM metrics exposed via JMX can be displayed on Ganglia using JMXTrans. Hence, JMXTrans acts as a bridge between Storm and Ganglia.

The following diagram shows how JMXTrans is used between the Storm node and Ganglia:

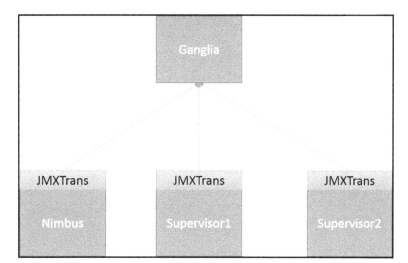

Perform the following steps to set up JMXTrans and Ganglia:

1. Run the following commands to download and install the JMXTrans tool on each Storm node:

```
wget https://jmxtrans.googlecode.com/files/jmxtrans-239-0.noarch.
rpm
sudo rpm -i jmxtrans-239-0.noarch.rpm
```

2. Run the following commands to install the Ganglia Gmond and Gmetad packages on any machine in a network. You can deploy the Gmetad and Gmond processes on a machine that will not be a part of the Storm cluster:

```
sudo yum -q -y install rrdtool
sudo yum -q -y install ganglia-gmond
sudo yum -q -y install ganglia-gmetad
sudo yum -q -y install ganglia-web
```

1. Edit the following line in the `gmetad.conf` configuration file, which is located at `/etc/ganglia` in the Gmetad process. We are editing this file to specify the name of the data source and the IP address of the Ganglia Gmetad machine:

```
data_source "stormcluster" 127.0.0.1
```

You can replace `127.0.0.1` with the IP address of the Ganglia Gmetad machine.

4. Edit the following line in the `gmond.conf` configuration file, which is located at `/etc/ganglia`, in the Gmond process:

```
cluster {
  name = "stormcluster"
  owner = "clusterOwner"
  latlong = "unspecified"
  url = "unspecified"
  }
host {
    location = "unspecified"
  }
udp_send_channel {
    host = 127.0.0.1
    port = 8649
    ttl = 1
  }
udp_recv_channel {
    port = 8649
  }
```

Here, `127.0.0.1` is the IP address of the Storm node. You need to replace `127.0.0.1` with the actual IP address of the machine. We have mainly edited the following entries in the Gmond configuration file:

- The cluster name
- The host address of the head Gmond node in the `udp_send` channel
- The port in the `udp_recv` channel

5. Edit the following line in the `ganglia.conf` file, which is located at `/etc/httpd/conf.d`. We are editing the `ganglia.conf` file to enable access on the Ganglia UI from all machines:

```
Alias /ganglia /usr/share/ganglia <Location /ganglia>Allow from all</Location>
```

The `ganglia.conf` file can be found on the node where the Ganglia web frontend application is installed. In our case, the Ganglia web interface and the Gmetad server are installed on the same machine.

6. Run the following commands to start the Ganglia Gmond, Gmetad, and web UI processes:

```
sudo service gmond start
setsebool -P httpd_can_network_connect 1
sudo service gmetad start
sudo service httpd stop
sudo service httpd start
```

7. Now, go to `http://127.0.0.1/ganglia` to verify the installation of Ganglia, and replace `127.0.0.1` with the IP address of the Ganglia web interface machine.

8. Now, you will need to write a `supervisor.json` file on each supervisor node to collect the JVM metrics of the Storm supervisor node using JMXTrans and then publish them on Ganglia using the `com.googlecode.jmxtrans.model.output.GangliaWriter OutputWriters` class. The `com.googlecode.jmxtrans.model.output.GangliaWriter OutputWriters` class is used to process the input JVM metrics and convert them into the format used by Ganglia. The following is the content for the `supervisor.json` JSON file:

```
{
  "servers" : [ {
    "port" : "12346",
    "host" : "IP_OF_SUPERVISOR_MACHINE",
    "queries" : [ {
      "outputWriters": [{
        "@class":
        "com.googlecode.jmxtrans.model.output.GangliaWriter",
"settings": {
          "groupName": "supervisor",
          "host": "IP_OF_GANGLIA_GMOND_SERVER",
          "port": "8649" }
      }],
      "obj": "java.lang:type=Memory",
      "resultAlias": "supervisor",
      "attr": ["ObjectPendingFinalizationCount"]
    },
    {
      "outputWriters": [{
        "@class":
        "com.googlecode.jmxtrans.model.output.GangliaWriter",
```

```
      "settings" {
            "groupName": " supervisor ",
            "host": "IP_OF_GANGLIA_GMOND_SERVER",
            "port": "8649"
         }
      }],
      "obj": "java.lang:name=Copy,type=GarbageCollector",
      "resultAlias": " supervisor ",
      "attr": [
        "CollectionCount",
        "CollectionTime"
      ]
    },
    {
      "outputWriters": [{
        "@class":
        "com.googlecode.jmxtrans.model.output.GangliaWriter",
      "settings": {
            "groupName": "supervisor ",
            "host": "IP_OF_GANGLIA_GMOND_SERVER",
            "port": "8649"
         }
      }],
      "obj": "java.lang:name=Code Cache,type=MemoryPool",
      "resultAlias": "supervisor ",
      "attr": [
        "CollectionUsageThreshold",
        "CollectionUsageThresholdCount",
        "UsageThreshold",
        "UsageThresholdCount"
      ]
    },
    {
      "outputWriters": [{
        "@class":
        "com.googlecode.jmxtrans.model.output.GangliaWriter",
      "settings": {
            "groupName": "supervisor ",
            "host": "IP_OF_GANGLIA_GMOND_SERVER",
            "port": "8649"
         }
      }],
      "obj": "java.lang:type=Runtime",
      "resultAlias": "supervisor",
      "attr": [
        "StartTime",
        "Uptime"
      ]
```

```
    }
    ],
    "numQueryThreads" : 2
  }]
}
```

Here, `12346` is the JMX port of the supervisor specified in the `storm.yaml` file.

You need to replace the `IP_OF_SUPERVISOR_MACHINE` value with the IP address of the supervisor machine. If you have two supervisors in a cluster, then the `supervisor.json` file of node 1 contains the IP address of node 1, and the `supervisor.json` file of node 2 contains the IP address of node 2.

You need to replace the `IP_OF_GANGLIA_GMOND_SERVER` value with the IP address of the Ganglia Gmond server.

9. Create the `nimbus.json` file on the Nimbus node. Using JMXTrans, collect the Storm Nimbus's process JVM metrics and publish them on Ganglia using the `com.googlecode.jmxtrans.model.output.GangliaWriter` `OutputWriters` class. The following are the contents of the `nimbus.json` file:

```
{
  "servers" : [{
    "port" : "12345",
    "host" : "IP_OF_NIMBUS_MACHINE",
    "queries" : [
      { "outputWriters": [{
        "@class":
        "com.googlecode.jmxtrans.model.output.GangliaWriter",
        "settings": {
          "groupName": "nimbus",
          "host": "IP_OF_GANGLIA_GMOND_SERVER",
          "port": "8649"
        }
      }],
      "obj": "java.lang:type=Memory",
      "resultAlias": "nimbus",
      "attr": ["ObjectPendingFinalizationCount"]
      },
      {
        "outputWriters": [{
          "@class":
          "com.googlecode.jmxtrans.model.output.GangliaWriter",
"settings": {
          "groupName": "nimbus",
          "host": "IP_OF_GANGLIA_GMOND_SERVER",
```

```
          "port": "8649"
        }
    }],
    "obj": "java.lang:name=Copy,type=GarbageCollector",
    "resultAlias": "nimbus",
    "attr": [
      "CollectionCount",
      "CollectionTime"
    ]
},
{
    "outputWriters": [{
      "@class":
      "com.googlecode.jmxtrans.model.output.GangliaWriter",
      "settings": {
        "groupName": "nimbus",
        "host": "IP_OF_GANGLIA_GMOND_SERVER",
        "port": "8649"
      }
    }],
    "obj": "java.lang:name=Code Cache,type=MemoryPool",
    "resultAlias": "nimbus",
    "attr": [
      "CollectionUsageThreshold",
      "CollectionUsageThresholdCount",
      "UsageThreshold",
      "UsageThresholdCount"
    ]
},
{
    "outputWriters": [{
      "@class":
      "com.googlecode.jmxtrans.model.output.GangliaWriter",
"settings": {
        "groupName": "nimbus",
        "host": "IP_OF_GANGLIA_GMOND_SERVER",
        "port": "8649"
      }
    }],
    "obj": "java.lang:type=Runtime",
    "resultAlias": "nimbus",
    "attr": [
      "StartTime",
      "Uptime"
    ]
  }
]
"numQueryThreads" : 2
```

```
    } ]
  }
```

Here, `12345` is the JMX port of the Nimbus machine specified in the `storm.yaml` file.

You need to replace the `IP_OF_NIMBUS_MACHINE` value with the IP address of the Nimbus machine.

You need to replace the `IP_OF_GANGLIA_GMOND_SERVER` value with the IP address of the Ganglia Gmond server.

10. Run the following commands on each Storm node to start the JMXTrans process:

```
cd /usr/share/jmxtrans/
sudo ./jmxtrans.sh start PATH_OF_JSON_FILES
```

Here, `PATH_OF_JSON_FILE` is the location of the `supervisor.json` and `nimbus.json` files.

11. Now, go to the Ganglia page at `http://127.0.0.1/ganglia` to view the Storm metrics. The following screenshot shows what the Storm metrics look like:

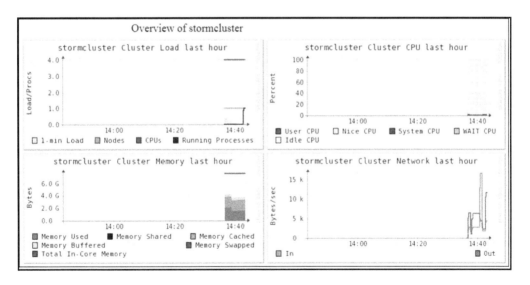

Perform the following steps to view the metrics of Storm Nimbus and the supervisor processed on the Ganglia UI:

1. Open the Ganglia page.
2. Now click on the `stormcluster` link to view the metrics of the Storm cluster.

The following screenshot shows the metrics of the Storm supervisor node:

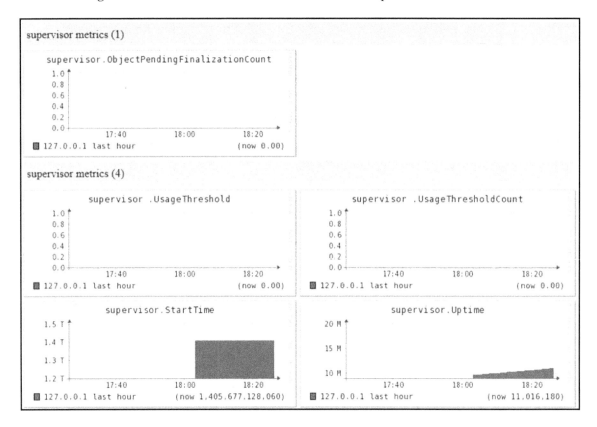

The following screenshot shows the metrics of the Storm Nimbus node:

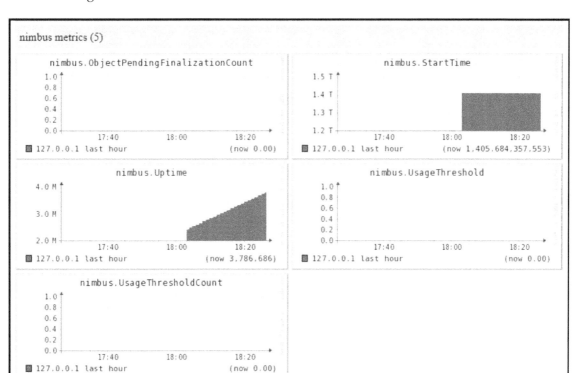

Summary

In this chapter, we covered the monitoring of the Storm cluster through the Nimbus thrift client--similar to what we covered through the Storm UI. We also covered how we can configure the Storm to publish the JMX metrics and the integration of Storm with Ganglia.

In the next chapter, we are going to cover the integration of Storm with Kafka and look at some sample examples to illustrate the process.

8
Integration of Storm and Kafka

Apache Kafka is a high-throughput, distributed, fault-tolerant, and replicated messaging system that was first developed at LinkedIn. The use cases of Kafka vary from log aggregation, to stream processing, to replacing other messaging systems.

Kafka has emerged as one of the important components of real-time processing pipelines in combination with Storm. Kafka can act as a buffer or feeder for messages that need to be processed by Storm. Kafka can also be used as the output sink for results emitted from Storm topologies.

In this chapter, we will be covering the following topics:

- Kafka architecture--broker, producer, and consumer
- Installation of the Kafka cluster
- Sharing the producer and consumer between Kafka
- Development of Storm topology using Kafka consumer as Storm spout
- Deployment of a Kafka and Storm integration topology

Introduction to Kafka

In this section we are going to cover the architecture of Kafka--broker, consumer, and producer.

Kafka architecture

Kafka has an architecture that differs significantly from other messaging systems. Kafka is a peer to peer system (each node in a cluster has the same role) in which each node is called a **broker**. The brokers coordinate their actions with the help of a ZooKeeper ensemble. The Kafka metadata managed by the ZooKeeper ensemble is mentioned in the section *Sharing ZooKeeper between Storm and Kafka*:

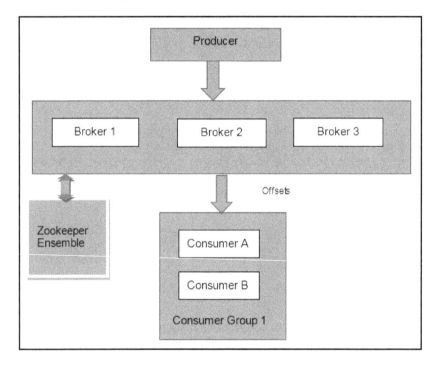

Figure 8.1: A Kafka cluster

The following are the important components of Kafka:

Producer

A producer is an entity that uses the Kafka client API to publish messages into the Kafka cluster. In a Kafka broker, messages are published by the producer entity to named entities called **topics**. A topic is a persistent queue (data stored into topics is persisted to disk).

For parallelism, a Kafka topic can have multiple partitions. Each partition data is represented in a different file. Also, two partitions of a single topic can be allocated on a different broker, thus increasing throughput as all partitions are independent of each other. Each message in a partition has a unique sequence number associated with it called an **offset**:

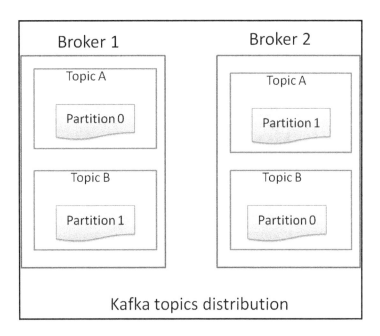

Figure 8.2: Kafka topic distribution

Replication

Kafka supports the replication of partitions of topics to support fault tolerance. Kafka automatically handles the replication of partitions and makes sure that the replica of a partition will be assigned to different brokers. Kafka elects one broker as the leader of a partition and all writes and reads must go to the partition leader. Replication features are introduced in Kafka 8.0.0 version.

The Kafka cluster manages the list of **in sync replica** (**ISR**)--the replicate which are in sync with the partition leader into ZooKeeper. If the partition leader goes down, then the followers/replicas that are present in the ISR list are only eligible for the next leader of the failed partition.

Consumer

Consumers read a range of messages from a broker. Each consumer has an assigned group ID. All the consumers with the same group ID act as a single logical consumer. Each message of a topic is delivered to one consumer from a consumer group (with the same group ID). Different consumer groups for a particular topic can process messages at their own pace as messages are not removed from the topics as soon as they are consumed. In fact, it is the responsibility of the consumers to keep track of how many messages they have consumed.

As mentioned earlier, each message in a partition has a unique sequence number associated with it called an offset. It is through this offset that consumers know how much of the stream they have already processed. If a consumer decides to replay already processed messages, all it needs to do is just set the value of an offset to an earlier value before consuming messages from Kafka.

Broker

The broker receives the messages from the producer (push mechanism) and delivers the messages to the consumer (pull mechanism). Brokers also manage the persistence of messages in a file. Kafka brokers are very lightweight: they only open file pointers on a queue (topic partitions) and manage TCP connections.

Data retention

Each topic in Kafka has an associated retention time. When this time expires, Kafka deletes the expired data file for that particular topic. This is a very efficient operation as it's a file delete operation.

Installation of Kafka brokers

At the time of writing, the stable version of Kafka is 0.9.x.

The prerequisites for running Kafka are a ZooKeeper ensemble and Java Version 1.7 or above. Kafka comes with a convenience script that can start a single node ZooKeeper but it is not recommended to use it in a production environment. We will be using the ZooKeeper cluster we deployed in `Chapter 2`, *Storm Deployment, Topology Development, and Topology Options*.

We will see how to set up a single node Kafka cluster first and then how to add two more nodes to it to run a full-fledged, three node Kafka cluster with replication enabled.

Setting up a single node Kafka cluster

Following are the steps to set up a single node Kafka cluster:

1. Download the Kafka 0.9.x binary distribution named `kafka_2.10-0.9.0.1.tar.gz` from `http://apache.claz.org/kafka/0.9.0.1/kafka_2.10-0.9.0.1.tgz`.

2. Extract the archive to wherever you want to install Kafka with the following command:

   ```
   tar -xvzf kafka_2.10-0.9.0.1.tgz
   cd kafka_2.10-0.9.0.1
   ```

   We will refer to the Kafka installation directory as `$KAFKA_HOME` from now on.

3. Change the following properties in the `$KAFKA_HOME/config/server.properties` file:

   ```
   log.dirs=/var/kafka-
   logszookeeper.connect=zoo1:2181,zoo2:2181,zoo3:2181
   ```

   Here, `zoo1`, `zoo2`, and `zoo3` represent the hostnames of the ZooKeeper nodes.

   The following are the definitions of the important properties in the `server.properties` file:

   - `broker.id`: This is a unique integer ID for each of the brokers in a Kafka cluster.
   - `port`: This is the port number for a Kafka broker. Its default value is `9092`. If you want to run multiple brokers on a single machine, give a unique port to each broker.
   - `host.name`: The hostname to which the broker should bind and advertise itself.

- `log.dirs`: The name of this property is a bit unfortunate as it represents not the log directory for Kafka, but the directory where Kafka stores the actual data sent to it. This can take a single directory or a comma-separated list of directories to store data. Kafka throughput can be increased by attaching multiple physical disks to the broker node and specifying multiple data directories, each lying on a different disk. It is not much use specifying multiple directories on the same physical disk, as all the I/O will still be happening on the same disk.
- `num.partitions`: This represents the default number of partitions for newly created topics. This property can be overridden when creating new topics. A greater number of partitions results in greater parallelism at the cost of a larger number of files.
- `log.retention.hours`: Kafka does not delete messages immediately after consumers consume them. It retains them for the number of hours defined by this property so that in the event of any issues the consumers can replay the messages from Kafka. The default value is `168` hours, which is 1 week.
- `zookeeper.connect`: This is the comma-separated list of ZooKeeper nodes in `hostname:port` form.

4. Start the Kafka server by running the following command:

```
> ./bin/kafka-server-start.sh config/server.properties
[2017-04-23 17:44:36,667] INFO New leader is 0
(kafka.server.ZookeeperLeaderElector$LeaderChangeListener)
[2017-04-23 17:44:36,668] INFO Kafka version : 0.9.0.1
(org.apache.kafka.common.utils.AppInfoParser)
[2017-04-23 17:44:36,668] INFO Kafka commitId : a7a17cdec9eaa6c5
(org.apache.kafka.common.utils.AppInfoParser)
[2017-04-23 17:44:36,670] INFO [Kafka Server 0], started
(kafka.server.KafkaServer)
```

If you get something similar to the preceding three lines on your console, then your Kafka broker is up-and-running and we can proceed to test it.

5. Now we will verify that the Kafka broker is set up correctly by sending and receiving some test messages. First, let's create a verification topic for testing by executing the following command:

```
> bin/kafka-topics.sh --zookeeper zoo1:2181 --replication-factor 1
--partition 1 --topic verification-topic --create
Created topic "verification-topic".
```

6. Now let's verify if the topic creation was successful by listing all the topics:

```
> bin/kafka-topics.sh --zookeeper zoo1:2181 --list
verification-topic
```

7. The topic is created; let's produce some sample messages for the Kafka cluster. Kafka comes with a command-line producer that we can use to produce messages:

```
> bin/kafka-console-producer.sh --broker-list localhost:9092 --
topic verification-topic
```

8. Write the following messages on your console:

```
Message 1
Test Message 2
Message 3
```

9. Let's consume these messages by starting a new console consumer on a new console window:

```
> bin/kafka-console-consumer.sh --zookeeper localhost:2181 --topic
verification-topic --from-beginning
Message 1
Test Message 2
Message 3
```

Now, if we enter any message on the producer console, it will automatically be consumed by this consumer and displayed on the command line.

Using Kafka's single node ZooKeeper

If you don't want to use an external ZooKeeper ensemble, you can use the single node ZooKeeper instance that comes with Kafka for quick and dirty development. To start using it, first modify the `$KAFKA_HOME/config/zookeeper.properties` file to specify the data directory by supplying following property:
`dataDir=/var/zookeeper`
Now, you can start the Zookeeper instance with the following command:
`> ./bin/zookeeper-server-start.sh config/zookeeper.properties`

Setting up a three node Kafka cluster

So far we have a single node Kafka cluster. Follow the steps to deploy the Kafka cluster:

1. Create a three node VM or three physical machines.
2. Perform steps 1 and 2 mentioned in the section *Setting up a single node Kafka cluster*.
3. Change the following properties in the file `$KAFKA_HOME/config/server.properties`:

   ```
   broker.id=0
   port=9092
   host.name=kafka1
   log.dirs=/var/kafka-logs
   zookeeper.connect=zoo1:2181,zoo2:2181,zoo3:2181
   ```

   Make sure that the value of the `broker.id` property is unique for each Kafka broker and the value of `zookeeper.connect` must be the same on all nodes.

4. Start the Kafka brokers by executing the following command on all three boxes:

   ```
   > ./bin/kafka-server-start.sh config/server.properties
   ```

5. Now let's verify the setup. First we create a topic with the following command:

   ```
   > bin/kafka-topics.sh --zookeeper zoo1:2181 --replication-factor 4
   --partition 1 --topic verification --create
      Created topic "verification-topic".
   ```

6. Now, we will list the topics to see if the topic was created successfully:

```
> bin/kafka-topics.sh --zookeeper zoo1:2181 --list
                topic: verification    partition: 0    leader: 0
replicas: 0              isr: 0
                topic: verification    partition: 1    leader: 1
replicas: 1              isr: 1
                topic: verification    partition: 2    leader: 2
replicas: 2              isr: 2
```

7. Now, we will verify the setup by using the Kafka console producer and consumer as done in the *Setting up a single node Kafka cluster* section:

```
> bin/kafka-console-producer.sh --broker-list
kafka1:9092,kafka2:9092,kafka3:9092 --topic verification
```

8. Write the following messages on your console:

```
First
Second
Third
```

9. Let's consume these messages by starting a new console consumer on a new console window:

```
> bin/kafka-console-consumer.sh --zookeeper localhost:2181 --topic
verification --from-beginning
First
Second
Third
```

So far, we have three brokers on the Kafka cluster working. In the next section, we will see how to write a producer that can produce messages to Kafka:

Multiple Kafka brokers on a single node

If you want to run multiple Kafka brokers on a single node, then follow the following steps:

1. Copy `config/server.properties` to create `config/server1.properties` and `config/server2.properties`.

2. Populate the following properties in `config/server.properties`:

```
broker.id=0
port=9092
log.dirs=/var/kafka-logs
zookeeper.connect=zoo1:2181,zoo2:2181,zoo3:2181
```

3. Populate the following properties in `config/server1.properties`:

```
broker.id=1
port=9093
log.dirs=/var/kafka-1-logs
zookeeper.connect=zoo1:2181,zoo2:2181,zoo3:2181
```

4. Populate the following properties in `config/server2.properties`:

```
broker.id=2
port=9094
log.dirs=/var/kafka-2-logs
zookeeper.connect=zoo1:2181,zoo2:2181,zoo3:2181
```

5. Run the following commands on three different terminals to start Kafka brokers:

```
> ./bin/kafka-server-start.sh config/server.properties
> ./bin/kafka-server-start.sh config/server1.properties
> ./bin/kafka-server-start.sh config/server2.properties
```

Share ZooKeeper between Storm and Kafka

We can share the same ZooKeeper ensemble between Kafka and Storm as both store the metadata inside the different znodes (ZooKeeper coordinates between the distributed processes using the shared hierarchical namespace, which is organized similarly to a standard file system. In ZooKeeper, the namespace consisting of data registers is called znodes).

We need to open the ZooKeeper client console to view the znodes (shared namespace) created for Kafka and Storm.

Go to `ZK_HOME` and execute the following command to open the ZooKeeper console:

```
> bin/zkCli.sh
```

Execute the following command to view the list of znodes:

```
> [zk: localhost:2181(CONNECTED) 0] ls /
[storm, consumers, isr_change_notification, zookeeper, admin, brokers]
```

Here, consumers, `isr_change_notification`, and brokers are the znodes and the Kafka is managing its metadata information into ZooKeeper at this location.

Storm manages its metadata inside the Storm znodes in ZooKeeper.

Kafka producers and publishing data into Kafka

In this section we are writing a Kafka producer that will publish events into the Kafka topic.

Perform the following step to create the producer:

1. Create a Maven project by using `com.stormadvance` as `groupId` and `kafka-producer` as `artifactId`.
2. Add the following dependencies for Kafka in the `pom.xml` file:

```xml
<dependency>
  <groupId>org.apache.kafka</groupId>
  <artifactId>kafka_2.10</artifactId>
  <version>0.9.0.1</version>
  <exclusions>
    <exclusion>
      <groupId>com.sun.jdmk</groupId>
      <artifactId>jmxtools</artifactId>
    </exclusion>
    <exclusion>
      <groupId>com.sun.jmx</groupId>
      <artifactId>jmxri</artifactId>
    </exclusion>
  </exclusions>
</dependency>
<dependency>
  <groupId>org.apache.logging.log4j</groupId>
  <artifactId>log4j-slf4j-impl</artifactId>
  <version>2.0-beta9</version>
</dependency>
<dependency>
  <groupId>org.apache.logging.log4j</groupId>
  <artifactId>log4j-1.2-api</artifactId>
```

```
      <version>2.0-beta9</version>
    </dependency>
```

3. Add the following `build` plugins to the `pom.xml` file. It will let us execute the producer using Maven:

```
<build>
  <plugins>
    <plugin>
      <groupId>org.codehaus.mojo</groupId>
      <artifactId>exec-maven-plugin</artifactId>
      <version>1.2.1</version>
      <executions>
        <execution>
          <goals>
            <goal>exec</goal>
          </goals>
        </execution>
      </executions>
      <configuration>
        <executable>java</executable>
<includeProjectDependencies>true</includeProjectDependencies
<includePluginDependencies>false</includePluginDependencies>
        <classpathScope>compile</classpathScope>
        <mainClass>com.stormadvance.kafka_producer.
KafkaSampleProducer
        </mainClass>
      </configuration>
    </plugin>
  </plugins>
</build>
```

4. Now we will create the `KafkaSampleProducer` class in the `com.stormadvance.kafka_producer` package. This class will produce each word from the first paragraph of Franz Kafka's Metamorphosis into the `new_topic` topic in Kafka as single message. The following is the code for the `KafkaSampleProducer` class with explanations:

```
public class KafkaSampleProducer {
  public static void main(String[] args) {
    // Build the configuration required for connecting to Kafka
    Properties props = new Properties();

    // List of kafka borkers. Complete list of brokers is not
required as
    // the producer will auto discover the rest of the brokers.
    props.put("bootstrap.servers", "Broker1-IP:9092");
```

```
    props.put("batch.size", 1);
    // Serializer used for sending data to kafka. Since we are
sending string,
    // we are using StringSerializer.
    props.put("key.serializer",
"org.apache.kafka.common.serialization.StringSerializer");
    props.put("value.serializer",
"org.apache.kafka.common.serialization.StringSerializer");

    props.put("producer.type", "sync");
    // Create the producer instance
    Producer<String, String> producer = new KafkaProducer<String,
String>(props);

    // Now we break each word from the paragraph
    for (String word : METAMORPHOSIS_OPENING_PARA.split("\\s")) {
      System.out.println("word : " + word);
      // Create message to be sent to "new_topic" topic with the
word
      ProducerRecord<String, String> data = new
ProducerRecord<String, String>("new_topic",word, word);
      // Send the message
      producer.send(data);
    }

    // close the producer
    producer.close();
    System.out.println("end : ");
  }

  // First paragraph from Franz Kafka's Metamorphosis
  private static String METAMORPHOSIS_OPENING_PARA = "One morning,
when Gregor Samsa woke from troubled dreams, he found "
              + "himself transformed in his bed into a horrible
vermin.  He lay on "
              + "his armour-like back, and if he lifted his head a
little he could "
              + "see his brown belly, slightly domed and divided
by arches into stiff "
              + "sections.  The bedding was hardly able to cover
it and seemed ready "
              + "to slide off any moment.  His many legs,
pitifully thin compared "
              + "with the size of the rest of him, waved about
helplessly as he "
              + "looked.";

}
```

5. Now, before running the producer, we need to create `new_topic` in Kafka. To do so, execute the following command:

```
> bin/kafka-topics.sh --zookeeper ZK1:2181 --replication-factor 1 -
-partition 1 --topic new_topic --create
Created topic "new_topic1".
```

6. Now we can run the producer by executing the following command:

```
> mvn compile exec:java
......
103  [com.learningstorm.kafka.WordsProducer.main()] INFO
kafka.client.ClientUti
ls$  - Fetching metadata from broker
id:0,host:kafka1,port:9092 with correlation id 0 for 1
topic(s) Set(words_topic)
110  [com.learningstorm.kafka.WordsProducer.main()] INFO
kafka.producer.SyncProducer  - Connected to kafka1:9092 for
producing
140  [com.learningstorm.kafka.WordsProducer.main()] INFO
kafka.producer.SyncProducer  - Disconnecting from
kafka1:9092
177  [com.learningstorm.kafka.WordsProducer.main()] INFO
kafka.producer.SyncProducer  - Connected to kafka1:9092 for
producing
378  [com.learningstorm.kafka.WordsProducer.main()] INFO
kafka.producer.Producer  - Shutting down producer
378  [com.learningstorm.kafka.WordsProducer.main()] INFO
kafka.producer.ProducerPool  - Closing all sync producers
381  [com.learningstorm.kafka.WordsProducer.main()] INFO
kafka.producer.SyncProducer  - Disconnecting from
kafka1:9092
```

7. Now let us verify that the message has been produced by using Kafka's console consumer and executing the following command:

```
> bin/kafka-console-consumer.sh --zookeeper ZK:2181 --topic
verification --from-beginning
                One
                morning,
                when
                Gregor
                Samsa
                woke
                from
                troubled
                dreams,
```

```
he
found
himself
transformed
in
his
bed
into
a
horrible
vermin.
. . . . . .
```

So, we are able to produce messages into Kafka. In the next section, we will see how we can use `KafkaSpout` to read messages from Kafka and process them inside a Storm topology.

Kafka Storm integration

Now we will create a Storm topology that will consume messages from the Kafka topic `new_topic` and aggregate words into sentences.

The complete message flow is shown as follows:

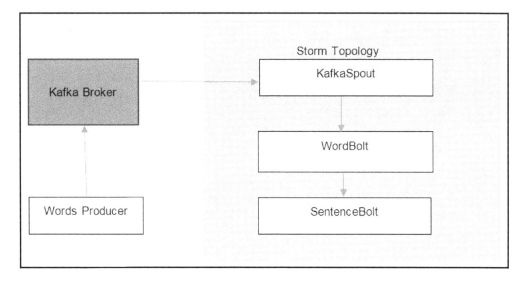

We have already seen `KafkaSampleProducer`, which produces words into the Kafka broker. Now we will create a Storm topology that will read those words from Kafka to aggregate them into sentences. For this, we will have one `KafkaSpout` in the application that will read the messages from Kafka and two bolts, `WordBolt` that receive words from `KafkaSpout` and then aggregate them into sentences, which are then passed onto the `SentenceBolt`, which simply prints them on the output stream. We will be running this topology in a local mode.

Follow the steps to create the Storm topology:

1. Create a new Maven project with `groupId` as `com.stormadvance` and `artifactId` as `kafka-storm-topology`.

2. Add the following dependencies for Kafka-Storm and Storm in the `pom.xml` file:

```
<dependency>
  <groupId>org.apache.storm</groupId>
  <artifactId>storm-kafka</artifactId>
  <version>1.0.2</version>
  <exclusions>
    <exclusion>
      <groupId>org.apache.kafka</groupId>
      <artifactId>kafka-clients</artifactId>
    </exclusion>
  </exclusions>
</dependency>

<dependency>
  <groupId>org.apache.kafka</groupId>
  <artifactId>kafka_2.10</artifactId>
  <version>0.9.0.1</version>
  <exclusions>
    <exclusion>
      <groupId>com.sun.jdmk</groupId>
      <artifactId>jmxtools</artifactId>
    </exclusion>
    <exclusion>
      <groupId>com.sun.jmx</groupId>
      <artifactId>jmxri</artifactId>
    </exclusion>
  </exclusions>
</dependency>

<dependency>
  <groupId>org.apache.storm</groupId>
  <artifactId>storm-core</artifactId>
  <version>1.0.2</version>
```

```
        <scope>provided</scope>
    </dependency>
    <dependency>
        <groupId>commons-collections</groupId>
        <artifactId>commons-collections</artifactId>
        <version>3.2.1</version>
    </dependency>

    <dependency>
        <groupId>com.google.guava</groupId>
        <artifactId>guava</artifactId>
        <version>15.0</version>
    </dependency>
```

3. Add the following Maven plugins to the `pom.xml` file so that we are able to run it from the command-line and also to package the topology to be executed in Storm:

```
<build>
  <plugins>
    <plugin>
      <artifactId>maven-assembly-plugin</artifactId>
      <configuration>
        <descriptorRefs>
          descriptorRef>jar-with-dependencies</descriptorRef>
        </descriptorRefs>
        <archive>
          <manifest>
            <mainClass></mainClass>
          </manifest>
        </archive>
      </configuration>
      <executions>
        <execution>
          <id>make-assembly</id>
          <phase>package</phase>
          <goals>
            <goal>single</goal>
          </goals>
        </execution>
      </executions>
    </plugin>

    <plugin>
      <groupId>org.codehaus.mojo</groupId>
      <artifactId>exec-maven-plugin</artifactId>
      <version>1.2.1</version>
      <executions>
        <execution>
```

```
            <goals>
              <goal>exec</goal>
            </goals>
          </execution>
        </executions>
        <configuration>
          <executable>java</executable>
<includeProjectDependencies>true</includeProjectDependencies
<includePluginDependencies>false</includePluginDependencies>
          <classpathScope>compile</classpathScope>
          <mainClass>${main.class}</mainClass>
        </configuration>
      </plugin>

      <plugin>
        <groupId>org.apache.maven.plugins</groupId>
        <artifactId>maven-compiler-plugin</artifactId>
      </plugin>

    </plugins>
  </build>
```

4. Now we will first create the `WordBolt` that will aggregate the words into sentences. For this, create a class called `WordBolt` in the `com.stormadvance.kafka` package. The code for `WordBolt` is as follows, complete with explanation:

```
public class WordBolt extends BaseBasicBolt {

  private static final long serialVersionUID =
  -5353547217135922477L;

  // list used for aggregating the words
  private List<String> words = new ArrayList<String>();

  public void execute(Tuple input, BasicOutputCollector collector)
  {
    System.out.println("called");
    // Get the word from the tuple
    String word = input.getString(0);

    if (StringUtils.isBlank(word)) {
      // ignore blank lines
      return;
    }

    System.out.println("Received Word:" + word);
```

```
        // add word to current list of words
        words.add(word);

        if (word.endsWith(".")) {
          // word ends with '.' which means this is // the end of the
sentence
          // publish a sentence tuple
          collector.emit(ImmutableList.of((Object)
StringUtils.join(words, ' ')));

          // reset the words list.
          words.clear();
        }
      }

    public void declareOutputFields(OutputFieldsDeclarer declarer) {
      // here we declare we will be emitting tuples with
      // a single field called "sentence"
      declarer.declare(new Fields("sentence"));
    }
  }
```

5. Next is `SentenceBolt`, which just prints the sentences that it receives. Create `SentenceBolt` in the `com.stormadvance.kafka` package. The code is as follows, with explanations:

```
public class SentenceBolt extends BaseBasicBolt {

  private static final long serialVersionUID =
7104400131657100876L;

  public void execute(Tuple input, BasicOutputCollector collector)
{
    // get the sentence from the tuple and print it
    System.out.println("Recieved Sentence:");
    String sentence = input.getString(0);
    System.out.println("Recieved Sentence:" + sentence);
  }

  public void declareOutputFields(OutputFieldsDeclarer declarer) {
        // we don't emit anything
  }
}
```

6. Now we will create the `KafkaTopology` that will define the `KafkaSpout` and wire it with `WordBolt` and `SentenceBolt`. Create a new class called `KafkaTopology` in the `com.stormadvance.kafka` package. The code is as follows, with explanations:

```
public class KafkaTopology {
  public static void main(String[] args) {
    try {
      // ZooKeeper hosts for the Kafka cluster
      BrokerHosts zkHosts = new ZkHosts("ZKIP:PORT");

      // Create the KafkaSpout configuartion
      // Second argument is the topic name
      // Third argument is the zookeepr root for Kafka
      // Fourth argument is consumer group id
      SpoutConfig kafkaConfig = new SpoutConfig(zkHosts,
"new_topic", "", "id1");

      // Specify that the kafka messages are String
      // We want to consume all the first messages in the topic
everytime
      // we run the topology to help in debugging. In production,
this
      // property should be false
      kafkaConfig.scheme = new SchemeAsMultiScheme(new
StringScheme());
      kafkaConfig.startOffsetTime =
kafka.api.OffsetRequest.EarliestTime();

      // Now we create the topology
      TopologyBuilder builder = new TopologyBuilder();

      // set the kafka spout class
      builder.setSpout("KafkaSpout", new KafkaSpout(kafkaConfig),
2);

      // set the word and sentence bolt class
      builder.setBolt("WordBolt", new WordBolt(),
1).globalGrouping("KafkaSpout");
      builder.setBolt("SentenceBolt", new SentenceBolt(),
1).globalGrouping("WordBolt");

      // create an instance of LocalCluster class for executing
topology
      // in local mode.
      LocalCluster cluster = new LocalCluster();
      Config conf = new Config();
```

```
        conf.setDebug(true);
        if (args.length > 0) {
          conf.setNumWorkers(2);
          conf.setMaxSpoutPending(5000);
          StormSubmitter.submitTopology("KafkaToplogy1", conf,
builder.createTopology());

        } else {
          // Submit topology for execution
          cluster.submitTopology("KafkaToplogy1", conf,
builder.createTopology());
          System.out.println("called1");
          Thread.sleep(1000000);
          // Wait for sometime before exiting
          System.out.println("Waiting to consume from kafka");

          System.out.println("called2");
          // kill the KafkaTopology
          cluster.killTopology("KafkaToplogy1");
          System.out.println("called3");
          // shutdown the storm test cluster
          cluster.shutdown();
        }

      } catch (Exception exception) {
        System.out.println("Thread interrupted exception : " +
exception);
      }
    }
}
```

7. Now we will the run the topology. Make sure the Kafka cluster is running and you have executed the producer in the last section so that there are messages in Kafka for consumption.

8. Run the topology by executing the following command:

```
> mvn clean compile exec:java  -
Dmain.class=com.stormadvance.kafka.KafkaTopology
```

This will execute the topology. You should see messages similar to the following in your output:

```
Recieved Word:One
Recieved Word:morning,
Recieved Word:when
Recieved Word:Gregor
Recieved Word:Samsa
```

```
Recieved Word:woke
Recieved Word:from
Recieved Word:troubled
Recieved Word:dreams,
Recieved Word:he
Recieved Word:found
Recieved Word:himself
Recieved Word:transformed
Recieved Word:in
Recieved Word:his
Recieved Word:bed
Recieved Word:into
Recieved Word:a
Recieved Word:horrible
Recieved Word:vermin.
Recieved Sentence:One morning, when Gregor Samsa woke from
troubled dreams, he found himself transformed in his bed
into a horrible vermin.
```

So we are able to consume messages from Kafka and process them in a Storm topology.

Deploy the Kafka topology on Storm cluster

The deployment of Kafka and Storm integration topology on the Storm cluster is similar to the deployment of other topologies. We need to set the number of workers and the maximum spout pending Storm config and we need to use the `submitTopology` method of `StormSubmitter` to submit the topology on the Storm cluster.

Now, we need to build the topology code as mentioned in the following steps to create a JAR of the Kafka Storm integration topology:

1. Go to project home.
2. Execute the command:

   ```
   mvn clean install
   ```

   The output of the preceding command is as follows:

   ```
   ------------------------------------------------------------
   -----
   [INFO] ------------------------------------------------------------
   -----
   [INFO] BUILD SUCCESS
   [INFO] ------------------------------------------------------------
   -----
   ```

```
[INFO] Total time: 58.326s
[INFO] Finished at:
[INFO] Final Memory: 14M/116M
[INFO] ------------------------------------------------------------
-----
```

3. Now, copy the Kafka Storm topology on the Nimbus machine and execute the following command to submit the topology on the Storm cluster:

```
bin/storm jar jarName.jar [TopologyMainClass] [Args]
```

The preceding command runs TopologyMainClass with the argument. The main function of TopologyMainClass is to define the topology and submit it to Nimbus. The Storm JAR part takes care of connecting to Nimbus and uploading the JAR part.

4. Log in on the Storm Nimbus machine and execute the following commands:

```
$> cd $STORM_HOME
$> bin/storm jar ~/storm-kafka-topology-0.0.1-SNAPSHOT-jar-with-
dependencies.jar com.stormadvance.kafka.KafkaTopology
KafkaTopology1
```

Here, ~/ storm-kafka-topology-0.0.1-SNAPSHOT-jar-with-dependencies.jar is the path of the KafkaTopology JAR we are deploying on the Storm cluster.

Summary

In this chapter, we learned about the basics of Apache Kafka and how to use it as part of a real-time stream processing pipeline build with Storm. We learned about the architecture of Apache Kafka and how it can be integrated into Storm processing by using KafkaSpout.

In the next chapter, we are going to cover the integration of Storm with Hadoop and YARN. We are also going to cover sample examples for this operation.

9
Storm and Hadoop Integration

So far, we have seen how Storm can be used for developing real-time stream processing applications. In general, these real-time applications are seldom used in isolation; they are more often than not used in combination with other batch processing operations.

The most common platform for developing batch jobs is Apache Hadoop. In this chapter, we will see how applications built with Apache Storm can be deployed over existing Hadoop clusters with the help of a Storm-YARN framework for optimized use and management of resources. We will also cover how we can write the process data into HDFS by creating an HDFS bolt in Storm.

In this chapter, we will cover the following topics:

- Overview of Apache Hadoop and its various components
- Setting up a Hadoop cluster
- Write Storm topology to persist data into HDFS
- Overview of Storm-YARN
- Deploying Storm-YARN on Hadoop
- Running a storm application on Storm-YARN.

Introduction to Hadoop

Apache Hadoop is an open source platform for developing and deploying big data applications. It was initially developed at Yahoo! based on the MapReduce and Google File System papers published by Google. Over the past few years, Hadoop has become the flagship big data platform.

In this section, we will discuss the key components of a Hadoop cluster.

Hadoop Common

This is the base library on which other Hadoop modules are based. It provides an abstraction for OS and filesystem operations so that Hadoop can be deployed on a variety of platforms.

Hadoop Distributed File System

Commonly known as **HDFS**, the **Hadoop Distributed File System** is a scalable, distributed, fault-tolerant filesystem. HDFS acts as the storage layer of the Hadoop ecosystem. It allows the sharing and storage of data and application code among the various nodes in a Hadoop cluster.

The following are the key assumptions taken while designing HDFS:

- It should be deployable on a cluster of commodity hardware.
- Hardware failures are expected, and it should be tolerant to these.
- It should be scalable to thousands of nodes.
- It should be optimized for high throughput, even at the cost of latency.
- Most of the files will be large in size, so it should be optimized for big files.
- Storage is cheap, so use replication for reliability.
- It should be locality aware so that the computations requested of the data can be performed on the physical node where it actually resides. This will result in less data movement, hence lower network congestion.

An HDFS cluster has the following components.

Namenode

The namenode is the master node in an HDFS cluster. It is responsible for managing the filesystem metadata and operations. It does not store any user data--but only the filesystem tree of all files in the cluster. It also keeps track of the physical locations of the blocks that are part of the files.

Since, the namenode keeps all the data in RAM, it should be deployed on a machine with a large amount of RAM. Also, no other processes should be hosted on the machine that is hosting the namenode so that all the resources are dedicated to it.

The namenode is the single point of failure in an HDFS cluster. If the namenode dies, no operations can take place on an HDFS cluster.

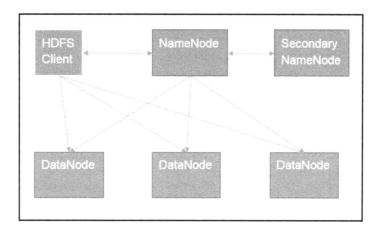

Figure 1: HDFS Cluster

Datanode

The datanode is responsible for storing user data in HDFS clusters. There can be multiple datanodes in an HDFS cluster. A datanode stores data on the physical disks attached to the system hosting the datanode. It is not recommended to store datanode data on disks in a RAID configuration as HDFS achieves data protection by replicating data across datanodes.

HDFS client

An HDFS client is a client library that can be used to interact with HDFS clusters. It usually talks to the namenode to perform meta operations, such as creating new files and so on, while the datanodes serve the actual data read and write requests.

Secondary namenode

The secondary namenode is one of the poorly named components of HDFS. Despite its name, it is not a standby for the namenode. To understand its function, we need to delve deep into how the namenode works.

A namenode keeps the filesystem metadata in the main memory. For durability, it also writes this metadata to the local disk in the form of the image file. When a namenode starts, it reads this fs image snapshot file to recreate the in-memory data structure for holding the filesystem data. Any updates on the filesystem are applied to the in-memory data structure, but not to the image. These changes are written to disk in separate files called edit logs. When a namenode starts, it merges these edit logs into the image so that the next restart will be quick. In production, the edit logs can grow very large as the namenode is not restarted frequently. This could result in a very long boot time for the namenode whenever it is restarted.

The secondary namenode is responsible for merging the edit logs of the namenode with the image so that the namenode starts faster the next time. It takes the image snapshot and the edit logs from the namenode and merges them and then puts the updated image snapshot on the namenode machines. This reduces the amount of merging that is required from the namenode on the restarts, thus reducing the time to boot for the namenode.

The following screenshot illustrates the working of the secondary namenode:

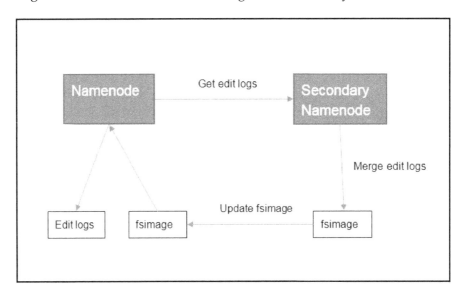

Figure 2: Secondary Namenode functioning

So far, we have seen the storage side of Hadoop. Next we will look into the processing components.

YARN

YARN is a cluster resource management framework that enables users to submit a variety of jobs to a Hadoop cluster, and manages scalability, fault tolerance, scheduling of jobs, and so on. As HDFS provides a storage layer for large amounts of data, the YARN framework gives you the plumbing required for writing big data processing applications.

The following are the major components of a YARN cluster.

ResourceManager (RM)

The ResourceManager is the entry point for applications in the YARN cluster. It is the master process in the cluster that is responsible for managing all the resources in the cluster. It is also responsible for the scheduling of various jobs submitted to the cluster. This scheduling policy is pluggable, and can be customized by a user in case they want to support new kinds of application.

NodeManager (NM)

A NodeManager agent is deployed on each of the processing nodes in the cluster. It is the counterpart to the ResourceManager at the node level. It communicates with the ResourceManager to update the node state and receive any job requests from it. It is also responsible for the life cycle management and the reporting of various node metrics to the ResourceManager.

ApplicationMaster (AM)

Once a job is scheduled by the ResourceManager, it no longer keeps track of its status and progress. This results in the ResourceManager being able to support completely different kinds of application in the cluster without worrying about the internal communication and logic of the application.

Whenever an application is submitted, the ResourceManager creates a new ApplicationMaster for that application, which is then responsible for negotiating resources from ResourceManager and communicating with the NodeMangers for the resources. NodeManager provides resources in the form of resource containers, which are abstractions for resource allocation, where you can tell how much CPU, memory, and so on is required.

Once the application starts running on various nodes in the cluster, the ApplicationMaster keeps track of the status of the various jobs and in case of failures, reruns those jobs. On completion of the job, it releases the resources to the ResourceManager.

The following screenshot illustrates the various components in a YARN cluster:

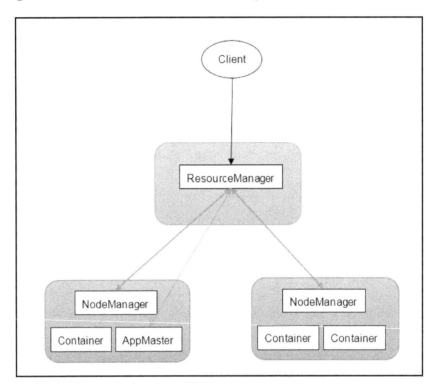

Figure 3: YARN components

Installation of Hadoop

Now that we have seen both the storage and processing parts of a Hadoop cluster, let's get started with the installation of Hadoop. We will be using Hadoop 2.2.0 in this chapter. Please note that this version is not compatible with Hadoop 1.X versions.

We will be setting up a cluster on a single node. Before starting, please make sure that you have the following installed on your system:

- JDK 1.7
- ssh-keygen

In case you don't have wget or ssh-keygen, install it with the following command:

```
# yum install openssh-clients
```

Next, we will need to set up a passwordless SSH on this machine as it is required for Hadoop.

Setting passwordless SSH

The following are the steps for setting up a passwordless SSH:

1. Generate your SSH key pair by executing the following command:

```
$ ssh-keygen -t rsa -P ''
Generating public/private rsa key pair.
Enter file in which to save the key (/home/anand/.ssh/id_rsa):
Your identification has been saved in /home/anand/.ssh/id_rsa.
Your public key has been saved in /home/anand/.ssh/id_rsa.pub.
The key fingerprint is:
b7:06:2d:76:ed:df:f9:1d:7e:5f:ed:88:93:54:0f:24
anand@localhost.localdomain
The key's randomart image is:
+--[ RSA 2048]----+
|                 |
|        E .      |
|         o      |
|      . .  o     |
|     S + .. o    |
|    . = o.   o|
|      o... .o|
|   .  oo.+*|
|       ..ooX|
+-----------------+
```

2. Next we need to copy the generated public key to the list of authorized keys in the current users. To do this, execute the following command:

```
$ cp ~/.ssh/id_rsa.pub ~/.ssh/authorized_keys
```

3. Now, we can check whether the passwordless SSH is working by connecting to localhost with the SSH by the following command:

```
$ ssh localhost
Last login: Wed Apr  2 09:12:17 2014 from localhost
```

Since we are able to use SSH into localhost without a password, our setup is working now and we will now proceed with the Hadoop setup.

Getting the Hadoop bundle and setting up environment variables

The following are the steps for setting up Hadoop:

1. Download Hadoop 2.2.0 from the Apache site at
   http://hadoop.apache.org/releases.html#Download.

2. Untar the archive at a location where we want to install Hadoop. We will call this
   location $HADOOP_HOME:

   ```
   $ tar xzf hadoop-2.2.0.tar.gz
   $ cd hadoop-2.2.0
   ```

3. Next, we need to set up the environment variables and the path for Hadoop, Add
   the following entries to your ~/.bashrc file. Make sure that you are providing
   the paths for Java and Hadoop as per your system:

   ```
   export JAVA_HOME=/usr/java/jdk1.7.0_45
   export HADOOP_HOME=/home/anand/opt/hadoop-2.2.0
   export HADOOP_COMMON_HOME=/home/anand/opt/hadoop-2.2.0
   export HADOOP_HDFS_HOME=$HADOOP_COMMON_HOME
   export HADOOP_MAPRED_HOME=$HADOOP_COMMON_HOME
   export HADOOP_YARN_HOME=$HADOOP_COMMON_HOME
   export HADOOP_CONF_DIR=$HADOOP_COMMON_HOME/etc/hadoop
   export HADOOP_COMMON_LIB_NATIVE_DIR=$HADOOP_COMMON_HOME/lib/native
   export HADOOP_OPTS="-Djava.library.path=$HADOOP_COMMON_HOME/lib"
   export
   PATH=$PATH:$JAVA_HOME/bin:$HADOOP_COMMON_HOME/bin:$HADOOP_COMMON_HOME/s
   bin
   ```

4. Refresh your ~/.bashrc file:

   ```
   $ source ~/.bashrc
   ```

5. Now let's check whether the paths are properly configured with the following command:

```
$ hadoop version
Hadoop 2.2.0
Subversion https://svn.apache.org/repos/asf/hadoop/common -r
1529768
Compiled by hortonmu on 2013-10-07T06:28Z
Compiled with protoc 2.5.0
From source with checksum 79e53ce7994d1628b240f09af91e1af4
This command was run using /home/anand/opt/hadoop-
2.2.0/share/hadoop/common/hadoop-common-2.2.0.jar
```

In the preceding snippet, we can see that the paths are properly set. Now we will set up HDFS on our system.

Setting up HDFS

Follow these steps for setting up HDFS:

1. Make directories for holding the namenode and datanode data:

```
$ mkdir -p ~/mydata/hdfs/namenode
$ mkdir -p ~/mydata/hdfs/datanode
```

2. Specify the namenode port in the $HADOOP_CONF_DIR/core-site.xml file by adding the following property inside the <configuration> tag:

```
<property>
        <name>fs.default.name</name>
        <value>hdfs://localhost:19000</value>
    <!-- The default port for HDFS is 9000, but we are using 19000 Storm-
Yarn uses port 9000 for its application master -->
</property>
```

3. Specify the namenode and datanode directory in the $HADOOP_CONF_DIR/hdfs-site.xml file by adding the following property inside the <configuration> tag:

```
<property>
        <name>dfs.replication</name>
        <value>1</value>
    <!-- Since we have only one node, we have replication factor=1 -->
</property>
<property>
```

```
            <name>dfs.namenode.name.dir</name>
            <value>file:/home/anand/hadoop-data/hdfs/namenode</value>
    <!-- specify absolute path of the namenode directory -->
</property>
<property>
            <name>dfs.datanode.data.dir</name>
            <value>file:/home/anand/hadoop-data/hdfs/datanode</value>
    <!-- specify absolute path of the datanode directory -->
</property>
```

4. Now we will format the namenode. This is a one-time process, and it needs to be done only while setting up the HDFS:

```
$ hdfs namenode -format
14/04/02 09:03:06 INFO namenode.NameNode: STARTUP_MSG:
/************************************************************
STARTUP_MSG: Starting NameNode
STARTUP_MSG:    host = localhost.localdomain/127.0.0.1
STARTUP_MSG:    args = [-format]
STARTUP_MSG:    version = 2.2.0
... ...
14/04/02 09:03:08 INFO namenode.NameNode: SHUTDOWN_MSG:
/************************************************************
SHUTDOWN_MSG: Shutting down NameNode at localhost.localdomain/127.0.0.1
************************************************************/
```

5. Now, we are done with the configuration, and we will start HDFS:

```
$ start-dfs.sh
14/04/02 09:27:13 WARN util.NativeCodeLoader: Unable to load native-
hadoop library for your platform... using builtin-java classes where
applicable
    Starting namenodes on [localhost]
    localhost: starting namenode, logging to
/home/anand/opt/hadoop-2.2.0/logs/hadoop-anand-namenode-
localhost.localdomain.out
    localhost: starting datanode, logging to
/home/anand/opt/hadoop-2.2.0/logs/hadoop-anand-datanode-
localhost.localdomain.out
    Starting secondary namenodes [0.0.0.0]
    0.0.0.0: starting secondarynamenode, logging to
/home/anand/opt/hadoop-2.2.0/logs/hadoop-anand-secondarynamenode-
localhost.localdomain.out
    14/04/02 09:27:32 WARN util.NativeCodeLoader: Unable to load native-
hadoop library for your platform... using builtin-java classes where
applicable
```

6. Now, execute the `jps` command to see if all the processes are running fine:

```
$ jps
50275 NameNode
50547 SecondaryNameNode
50394 DataNode
51091 Jps
```

Here, we can see that all the expected processes are running.

7. Now you can check the status of HDFS using the namenode UI by opening `http://localhost:50070` in your browser. You should see something similar to the following:

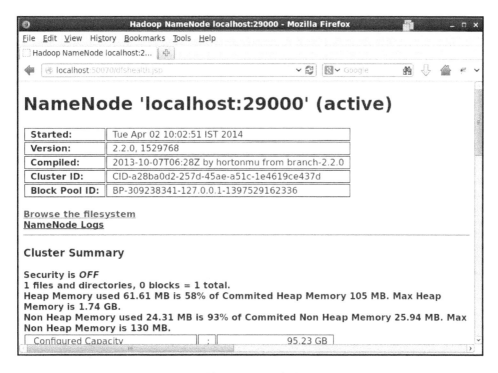

Figure 4: Namenode web UI

8. You can interact with HDFS using the `hdfs dfs` command. Get all the options by running `hdfs dfs` on a console or refer to the documentation at `http://hado op.apache.org/docs/r2.2.0/hadoop-project-dist/hadoop-common/FileSyst emShell.html`.

Now that HDFS is deployed, we will set up YARN next.

Setting up YARN

The following are the steps for setting up YARN:

1. Create a `mapred-site.xml` file from the template `mapred-site.xml.template`:

```
$ cp $HADOOP_CONF_DIR/mapred-site.xml.template
$HADOOP_CONF_DIR/mapred-
site.xml
```

2. Specify that we are using a YARN framework by adding the following property in the `$HADOOP_CONF_DIR/mapred-site.xml` file in the `<configuration>` tag:

```
<property>
        <name>mapreduce.framework.name</name>
        <value>yarn</value>
</property>
```

3. Configure the following properties in the `$HADOOP_CONF_DIR/yarn-site.xml` file:

```
<property>
        <name>yarn.nodemanager.aux-services</name>
        <value>mapreduce_shuffle</value>
</property>

<property>
        <name>yarn.scheduler.minimum-allocation-mb</name>
        <value>1024</value>
</property>

<property>
        <name>yarn.nodemanager.resource.memory-mb</name>
        <value>4096</value>
</property>

<property>
        <name>yarn.nodemanager.aux-
services.mapreduce.shuffle.class</name>
    <value>org.apache.hadoop.mapred.ShuffleHandler</value>
</property>
<property>
        <name>yarn.nodemanager.vmem-pmem-ratio</name>
        <value>8</value>
</property>
```

4. Start the YARN processes with the following command:

```
$ start-yarn.sh
starting yarn daemons
starting resourcemanager, logging to
/home/anand/opt/hadoop-2.2.0/logs/yarn-anand-resourcemanager-
localhost.localdomain.out
localhost: starting nodemanager, logging to
/home/anand/opt/hadoop-2.2.0/logs/yarn-anand-nodemanager-
localhost.localdomain.out
```

5. Now, execute the `jps` command to see if all the processes are running fine:

```
$ jps
50275 NameNode
50547 SecondaryNameNode
50394 DataNode
51091 Jps
50813 NodeManager
50716 ResourceManager
```

Here, we can see that all the expected processes are running.

6. Now you can check the status of YARN using the ResourceManager web UI by opening `http://localhost:8088/cluster` in your browser. You should see something similar to the following:

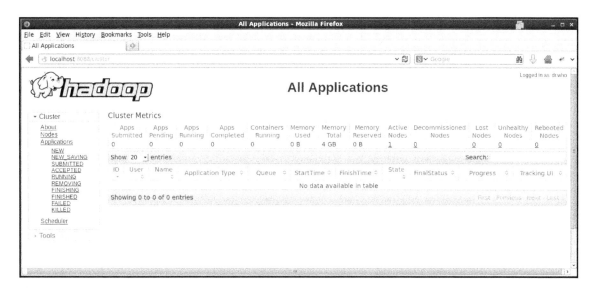

Figure 5: ResourceManager web UI

7. You can interact with YARN using the `yarn` command. Get all the options by running `yarn` on a console or refer to the documentation at `http://hadoop.apac he.org/docs/r2.2.0/hadoop-yarn/hadoop-yarn-site/YarnCommands.html`. To get all the applications currently running on YARN, run the following command:

```
$ yarn application -list
14/04/02 11:41:42 WARN util.NativeCodeLoader: Unable to load native-
hadoop library for your platform... using builtin-java classes where
applicable
    14/04/02 11:41:42 INFO client.RMProxy: Connecting to ResourceManager at
/0.0.0.0:8032
    Total number of applications (application-types: [] and states:
[SUBMITTED, ACCEPTED, RUNNING]):0
                    Application-Id        Application-Name
Application-Type        User        Queue                State
Final-State            Progress                    Tracking-URL
```

With this, we have completed the deployment of the Hadoop cluster on a single node. Next we will see how to run Storm topologies on this cluster.

Write Storm topology to persist data into HDFS

In this section, we are going to cover how we can write the HDFS bolt to persist data into HDFS. In this section, we are focusing on the following points:

- Consuming data from Kafka
- The logic to store the data into HDFS
- Rotating file into HDFS after a predefined time or size

Perform the following steps to create the topology to store the data into the HDFS:

1. Create a new maven project with groupId `com.stormadvance` and artifactId `storm-hadoop`.
2. Add the following dependencies in the `pom.xml` file. We are adding the Kafka Maven dependency in `pom.xml` to support Kafka Consumer. Please refer the previous chapter to produce data in Kafka as here we are going to consume data from Kafka and store in HDFS:

```
<dependency>
        <groupId>org.codehaus.jackson</groupId>
```

```xml
        <artifactId>jackson-mapper-asl</artifactId>
        <version>1.9.13</version>
</dependency>

<dependency>
        <groupId>org.apache.hadoop</groupId>
        <artifactId>hadoop-client</artifactId>
        <version>2.2.0</version>
        <exclusions>
                <exclusion>
                        <groupId>org.slf4j</groupId>
                        <artifactId>slf4j-log4j12</artifactId>
                </exclusion>
        </exclusions>
</dependency>
<dependency>
        <groupId>org.apache.hadoop</groupId>
        <artifactId>hadoop-hdfs</artifactId>
        <version>2.2.0</version>
        <exclusions>
                <exclusion>
                        <groupId>org.slf4j</groupId>
                        <artifactId>slf4j-log4j12</artifactId>
                </exclusion>
        </exclusions>
</dependency>
<!-- Dependency for Storm-Kafka spout -->
<dependency>
        <groupId>org.apache.storm</groupId>
        <artifactId>storm-kafka</artifactId>
        <version>1.0.2</version>
        <exclusions>
                <exclusion>
                        <groupId>org.apache.kafka</groupId>
                        <artifactId>kafka-clients</artifactId>
                </exclusion>
        </exclusions>
</dependency>

<dependency>
        <groupId>org.apache.kafka</groupId>
        <artifactId>kafka_2.10</artifactId>
        <version>0.9.0.1</version>
        <exclusions>
                <exclusion>
                        <groupId>com.sun.jdmk</groupId>
                        <artifactId>jmxtools</artifactId>
                </exclusion>
```

```
                        <exclusion>
                                <groupId>com.sun.jmx</groupId>
                                <artifactId>jmxri</artifactId>
                        </exclusion>
                </exclusions>
        </dependency>

        <dependency>
                <groupId>org.apache.storm</groupId>
                <artifactId>storm-core</artifactId>
                <version>1.0.2</version>
                <scope>provided</scope>
        </dependency>
</dependencies>
<repositories>
        <repository>
                <id>clojars.org</id>
                <url>http://clojars.org/repo</url>
        </repository>
</repositories>
```

3. Write a Storm Hadoop topology to consume data from HDFS and store it in HDFS. The following is a line-by-line description of the `com.stormadvance.storm_hadoop.topology.StormHDFSTopology` class:

4. Use the following lines to consume the data from Kafka:

```
// zookeeper hosts for the Kafka cluster
BrokerHosts zkHosts = new ZkHosts("localhost:2181");

// Create the KafkaReadSpout configuartion
// Second argument is the topic name
// Third argument is the zookeeper root for Kafka
// Fourth argument is consumer group id
SpoutConfig kafkaConfig = new SpoutConfig(zkHosts, "dataTopic",
"",
                "id7");

// Specify that the kafka messages are String
kafkaConfig.scheme = new SchemeAsMultiScheme(new StringScheme());

// We want to consume all the first messages in the topic everytime
// we run the topology to help in debugging. In production, this
// property should be false
kafkaConfig.startOffsetTime =
kafka.api.OffsetRequest.EarliestTime();
```

```
        // Now we create the topology
        TopologyBuilder builder = new TopologyBuilder();

        // set the kafka spout class
        builder.setSpout("KafkaReadSpout", new KafkaSpout(kafkaConfig),
1);
```

5. Use the following lines of code to define the HDFS Namenode details and the name of the HDFS data directory to store the data into HDFS, create a new file after every 5 MB chunk of data stored into HDFS, and sync the latest data into the file after every 1,000 records:

```
        // use "|" instead of "," for field delimiter
        RecordFormat format = new DelimitedRecordFormat()
                .withFieldDelimiter(",");

        // sync the filesystem after every 1k tuples
        SyncPolicy syncPolicy = new CountSyncPolicy(1000);

        // rotate files when they reach 5MB
        FileRotationPolicy rotationPolicy = new
FileSizeRotationPolicy(5.0f,
                Units.MB);

        FileNameFormat fileNameFormatHDFS = new DefaultFileNameFormat()
                .withPath("/hdfs-bolt-output/");

        HdfsBolt hdfsBolt2 = new
HdfsBolt().withFsUrl("hdfs://127.0.0.1:8020")
                .withFileNameFormat(fileNameFormatHDFS)
.withRecordFormat(format).withRotationPolicy(rotationPolicy)
                .withSyncPolicy(syncPolicy);
```

6. Use the following code to connect Spout with the HDFS bolt:

```
HdfsBolt hdfsBolt2 = new HdfsBolt().withFsUrl("hdfs://127.0.0.1:8020")
                .withFileNameFormat(fileNameFormatHDFS)
.withRecordFormat(format).withRotationPolicy(rotationPolicy)
                .withSyncPolicy(syncPolicy);
```

Integration of Storm with Hadoop

The probability that the organizations developing and operating big data applications already have a Hadoop cluster deployed is very high. Also, there is a high possibility that they also have real-time stream processing applications deployed to go along with the batch applications running on Hadoop.

It would be great if we can leverage the already deployed YARN cluster to also run the Storm topologies. This will reduce the operational cost of maintenance by giving you only one cluster to manage instead of two.

Storm-YARN is a project developed by Yahoo! that enables the deployment of Storm topologies over YARN clusters. It enables the deployment of Storm processes on nodes managed by YARN.

The following diagram illustrates how the Storm processes are deployed on YARN:

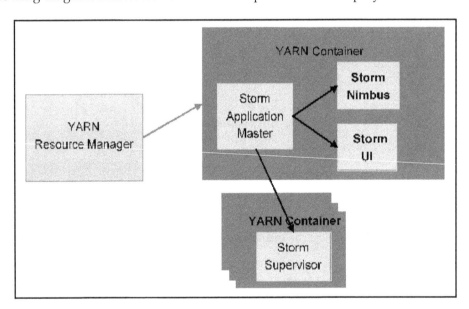

Figure 6: Storm processes on YARN

In the next section, we will see how to set up Storm-YARN.

Setting up Storm-YARN

Since Storm-YARN is still in alpha, we will be proceeding with the base master branch of the `git` repository. Make sure you have `git` installed on your system. If not, then run the following command:

```
# yum install git-core
```

Also make sure that you have Apache Zookeeper and Apache Maven installed on your system. Refer to the previous chapters for their setup instructions.

The following are the steps for deploying Storm-YARN:

1. Clone the `storm-yarn` repo with the following command:

   ```
   $ cd ~/opt
   $ git clone https://github.com/yahoo/storm-yarn.git
   $ cd storm-yarn
   ```

2. Build `storm-yarn` by running the following `mvn` command:

```
$ mvn package
[INFO] Scanning for projects...
[INFO]
[INFO] ------------------------------------------------------
[INFO] Building storm-yarn 1.0-alpha
[INFO] ------------------------------------------------------
...
[INFO] ------------------------------------------------------
[INFO] BUILD SUCCESS
[INFO] ------------------------------------------------------
[INFO] Total time: 32.049s
[INFO] Finished at: Fri Apr 04 09:45:06 IST 2014
[INFO] Final Memory: 14M/152M
[INFO] ------------------------------------------------------
```

3. Copy the `storm.zip` file from `storm-yarn/lib` to HDFS by using the following commands:

   ```
   $ hdfs dfs -mkdir -p  /lib/storm/1.0.2-wip21
   $ hdfs dfs -put lib/storm.zip /lib/storm/1.0.2-wip21/storm.zip
   ```

   The exact version might be different from `1.0.2-wip21` in your case.

4. Create a directory to hold our Storm configuration:

```
$ mkdir -p ~/storm-data
$ cp lib/storm.zip ~/storm-data/
$ cd ~/storm-data/
$ unzip storm.zip
```

5. Add the following configuration in the `~/storm-data/storm-1.0.2-wip21/conf/storm.yaml` file:

```
storm.zookeeper.servers:
    - "localhost"

nimbus.host: "localhost"

master.initial-num-supervisors: 2
master.container.size-mb: 128
```

If required, change the values as per your setup.

6. Add a `storm-yarn/bin` folder to your path by adding the following to the `~/.bashrc` file:

```
export PATH=$PATH:/home/anand/storm-data/storm-1.0.2-
wip21/bin:/home/anand/opt/storm-yarn/bin
```

7. Refresh `~/.bashrc`:

```
$ source ~/.bashrc
```

8. Make sure Zookeeper is running on your system. If not, then start ZooKeeper by running the following command:

```
$ ~/opt/zookeeper-3.4.5/bin/zkServer.sh start
```

9. Launch `storm-yarn` using the following command:

```
$ storm-yarn launch ~/storm-data/storm-1.0.2-wip21/conf/storm.yaml
14/04/15 10:14:49 INFO client.RMProxy: Connecting to ResourceManager at
/0.0.0.0:8032
14/04/15 10:14:49 INFO yarn.StormOnYarn: Copy App Master jar from local
filesystem and add to local environment
... ...
14/04/15 10:14:51 INFO impl.YarnClientImpl: Submitted application
application_1397537047058_0001 to ResourceManager at /0.0.0.0:8032
application_1397537047058_0001
```

The Storm-YARN application has been submitted with the application ID `application_1397537047058_0001`.

10. We can retrieve the status of our application by using the following `yarn` command:

```
$ yarn application -list
14/04/15 10:23:13 INFO client.RMProxy: Connecting to ResourceManager at
/0.0.0.0:8032
    Total number of applications (application-types: [] and states:
[SUBMITTED, ACCEPTED, RUNNING]):1
                    Application-Id          Application-Name
Application-Type            User        Queue                State
Final-State            Progress                        Tracking-URL
    application_1397537047058_0001              Storm-on-Yarn
YARN          anand      default            RUNNING            UNDEFINED
50%                                N/A
```

11. We can also see `storm-yarn` running on the ResourceManager web UI at `http://localhost:8088/cluster/`. You should be able to see something similar to the following:

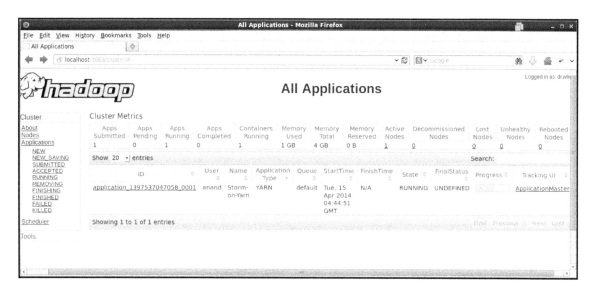

Figure 7: Storm-YARN on the ResourceManager web UI

You can explore the various metrics exposed by clicking through various links on the UI.

12. Nimbus should also be running now, and you should be able to see it through the Nimbus web UI at `http://localhost:7070/`:

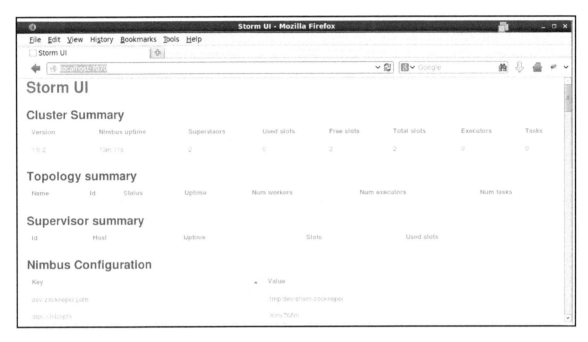

Figure 8: Nimbus web UI running on YARN

13. Now we need to get the Storm configuration that will be used when deploying topologies on this Storm cluster on YARN. To do so, execute the following command:

```
$ mkdir ~/.storm
$ storm-yarn getStormConfig --appId application_1397537047058_0001 --
output ~/.storm/storm.yaml
    14/04/15 10:32:01 INFO client.RMProxy: Connecting to ResourceManager at
/0.0.0.0:8032
    14/04/15 10:32:02 INFO yarn.StormOnYarn: application report for
application_1397537047058_0001 :localhost.localdomain:9000
    14/04/15 10:32:02 INFO yarn.StormOnYarn: Attaching to
localhost.localdomain:9000 to talk to app master
application_1397537047058_0001
    14/04/15 10:32:02 INFO yarn.StormMasterCommand: storm.yaml downloaded
into /home/anand/.storm/storm.yaml
```

Make sure that you are passing the correct application ID (as retrieved in step 9) to the `-appId` parameter.

Now that we have successfully deployed Storm-YARN, we will see how to run our topologies on this storm cluster.

Storm-Starter topologies on Storm-YARN

In this section, we will see how to deploy the Storm-Starter topologies on storm-yarn. Storm-Starter is a set of example topologies that comes with Storm.

Follow these steps to run the topologies on Storm-YARN:

1. Clone the storm-starter project:

   ```
   $ git clone https://github.com/nathanmarz/storm-starter
   $ cd storm-starter
   ```

2. Package the topologies with the following mvn command:

   ```
   $ mvn package -DskipTests
   ```

3. Deploy the topologies on storm-yarn with the following command:

   ```
   $ storm jar target/storm-starter-0.0.1-SNAPSHOT.jar
   storm.starter.WordCountTopology word-cout-topology
       545  [main] INFO  backtype.storm.StormSubmitter - Jar not uploaded to
   master yet. Submitting jar...
       558  [main] INFO  backtype.storm.StormSubmitter - Uploading topology
   jar target/storm-starter-0.0.1-SNAPSHOT.jar to assigned location: storm-
   local/nimbus/inbox/stormjar-9ab704ff-29f3-4b9d-b0ac-e9e41d4399dd.jar
       609  [main] INFO  backtype.storm.StormSubmitter - Successfully uploaded
   topology jar to assigned location: storm-
   local/nimbus/inbox/stormjar-9ab704ff-29f3-4b9d-b0ac-e9e41d4399dd.jar
       609  [main] INFO  backtype.storm.StormSubmitter - Submitting topology
   word-cout-topology in distributed mode with conf
   {"topology.workers":3,"topology.debug":true}
       937  [main] INFO  backtype.storm.StormSubmitter - Finished submitting
   topology: word-cout-topology
   ```

4. Now we can see the deployed topology on the Nimbus web UI at
   `http://localhost:7070/`:

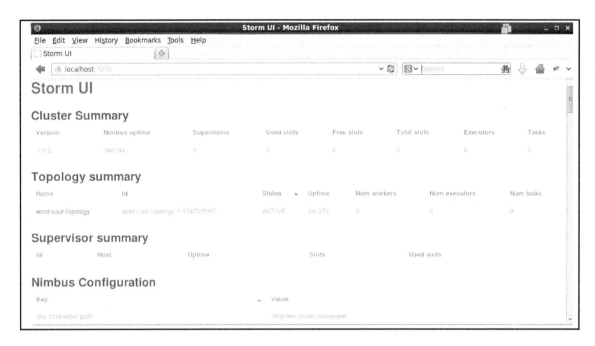

Figure 9: Nimbus web UI showing the word-count topology on YARN

5. To see how you can interact with the topologies running on `storm-yarn`, run the
   following command:

```
$ storm-yarn
```

6. It will list all the options interacting with the various Storm processes and
   starting new supervisors.

So in this section, we built a Storm-started topology and ran it on `storm-yarn`.

Summary

In this chapter, we introduced Apache Hadoop and the various components, such as HDFS, YARN, and so on, that are part of a Hadoop cluster. We also saw the subcomponents of an HDFS and YARN cluster and how they interact with each other. Then we walked through how to set up a single node Hadoop cluster.

We also introduced Storm-YARN, which was the main point of this chapter. Storm-YARN enables you to run Storm topologies on a Hadoop cluster. This helps from a manageability and operations point of view. Finally, we saw how to deploy a topology on Storm running on YARN.

In the next chapter, we will see how Storm can integrate with other big data technologies, such as HBase, Redis, and so on.

10
Storm Integration with Redis, Elasticsearch, and HBase

In the previous chapter, we covered an overview of Apache Hadoop and its various components. We also presented an overview of Storm-YARN, and looked at deploying Storm-YARN on Apache Hadoop.

In this chapter, we will explain how you can integrate Storm with other databases for storing the data, and how we can use Esper inside a Storm bolt to support the windowing operation.

The following are the key points we are going to cover in this chapter:

- Integration of Storm with HBase
- Integration of Storm with Redis
- Integration of Storm with Elasticsearch
- Integration of Storm with Esper to perform the windowing operation

Integrating Storm with HBase

As explained in earlier chapters, Storm is meant for real-time data processing. However, in most cases, you will need to store the processed data in a data store so that you can use the stored data for further batch analysis and execute the batch analysis query on the data stored. This section explains how you can store the data processed by Storm in HBase.

Before going to the implementation, I want to give a little overview of what HBase is. HBase is a NoSQL, multidimensional, sparse, horizontally scalable database that is modeled after **Google BigTable**. HBase is built on top of Hadoop, which means it relies on Hadoop and integrates with the MapReduce framework very well. Hadoop provides the following benefits to HBase:

- A distributed data store that runs on top of the commodity hardware
- Fault tolerance

We will assume that you have HBase installed and running on your system. You can refer to the article on HBase installation at `https://hbase.apache.org/cygwin.html`.

We will create a sample Storm topology that shows how you can store the data processed by Storm to HBase using the following steps:

1. Create a Maven project using `com.stormadvance` for the group ID and `stormhbase` for the artifact ID.
2. Add the following dependencies and repositories to the `pom.xml` file:

```
<repositories>
    <repository>
        <id>clojars.org</id>
        <url>http://clojars.org/repo</url>
    </repository>
</repositories>
<dependencies>
    <dependency>
        <groupId>org.apache.storm</groupId>
        <artifactId>storm-core</artifactId>
        <version>1.0.2</version>
        <scope>provided</scope>
    </dependency>
    <dependency>
        <groupId>org.apache.hadoop</groupId>
        <artifactId>hadoop-core</artifactId>
        <version>1.1.1</version>
    </dependency>
    <dependency>
        <groupId>org.slf4j</groupId>
        <artifactId>slf4j-api</artifactId>
        <version>1.7.7</version>
    </dependency>

    <dependency>
        <groupId>org.apache.hbase</groupId>
```

```
            <artifactId>hbase</artifactId>
            <version>0.94.5</version>
            <exclusions>
                <exclusion>
                    <artifactId>zookeeper</artifactId>
                    <groupId>org.apache.zookeeper</groupId>
                </exclusion>


            </exclusions>
        </dependency>

        <dependency>
            <groupId>junit</groupId>
            <artifactId>junit</artifactId>
            <version>4.10</version>
        </dependency>
    </dependencies>
    <build>
        <plugins>
            <plugin>
                <groupId>org.apache.maven.plugins</groupId>
                <artifactId>maven-compiler-plugin</artifactId>
                <version>2.5.1</version>
                <configuration>
                    <source>1.6</source>
                    <target>1.6</target>
                </configuration>
            </plugin>
            <plugin>
                <artifactId>maven-assembly-plugin</artifactId>
                <version>2.2.1</version>
                <configuration>
                    <descriptorRefs>
                        <descriptorRef>jar-
                        with-dependencies</descriptorRef>
                    </descriptorRefs>
                    <archive>
                        <manifest>
                            <mainClass />
                        </manifest>
                    </archive>
                </configuration>
                <executions>
                    <execution>
                        <id>make-assembly</id>
                        <phase>package</phase>
                        <goals>
```

```
                    <goal>single</goal>
                </goals>
            </execution>
        </executions>
    </plugin>
  </plugins>
</build>
```

3. Create an HBaseOperations class in the com.stormadvance.stormhbase
   package. The HBaseOperations class contains two methods:
   - createTable(String tableName, List<String>
     ColumnFamilies): This method takes the name of the table and the
     HBase column family list as input to create a table in HBase.
   - insert(Map<String, Map<String, Object>> record, String
     rowId): This method takes the record and its rowID parameter as
     input and inserts the input record to HBase. The following is the
     structure of the input record:

   ```
   {

     "columnfamily1":
     {
       "column1":"abc",
       "column2":"pqr"
     },
     "columnfamily2":
     {
       "column3":"bc",
       "column4":"jkl"
     }
   }
   ```

   Here, columnfamily1 and columnfamily2 are the names of HBase column
   families, and column1, column2, column3, and column4 are the names of
   columns.

   The rowId parameter is the HBase table row key that is used to uniquely
   identify each record in HBase.

The following is the source code of the `HBaseOperations` class:

```
public class HBaseOperations implements Serializable{

    private static final long serialVersionUID = 1L;

    // Instance of Hadoop Cofiguration class
    Configuration conf = new Configuration();
    HTable hTable = null;
    public HBaseOperations(String tableName, List<String>
ColumnFamilies,
            List<String> zookeeperIPs, int zkPort) {
        conf = HBaseConfiguration.create();
        StringBuffer zookeeperIP = new StringBuffer();
        // Set the zookeeper nodes
        for (String zookeeper : zookeeperIPs) {
            zookeeperIP.append(zookeeper).append(",");
        }
        zookeeperIP.deleteCharAt(zookeeperIP.length() - 1);

        conf.set("hbase.zookeeper.quorum",
zookeeperIP.toString());
        // Set the zookeeper client port
        conf.setInt("hbase.zookeeper.property.clientPort",
zkPort);
        // call the createTable method to create a table into
HBase.
        createTable(tableName, ColumnFamilies);
        try {
            // initilaize the HTable.
            hTable = new HTable(conf, tableName);
        } catch (IOException e) {
            throw new RuntimeException("Error occure while
creating instance of HTable class : " + e);
        }
    }

    /**
     * This method create a table into HBase
     *
     * @param tableName
     *                 Name of the HBase table
     * @param ColumnFamilies
     *                 List of column famallies
     *
     */
    public void createTable(String tableName, List<String>
ColumnFamilies) {
```

```
            HBaseAdmin admin = null;
        try {
            admin = new HBaseAdmin(conf);
            // Set the input table in HTableDescriptor
            HTableDescriptor tableDescriptor = new
HTableDescriptor(
                    Bytes.toBytes(tableName));
            for (String columnFamaliy : ColumnFamilies) {
                HColumnDescriptor columnDescriptor = new
HColumnDescriptor(
                        columnFamaliy);
                // add all the HColumnDescriptor into
HTableDescriptor
                tableDescriptor.addFamily(columnDescriptor);
            }
            /* execute the creaetTable(HTableDescriptor
tableDescriptor) of HBaseAdmin
             * class to createTable into HBase.
             */
            admin.createTable(tableDescriptor);
            admin.close();
        }catch (TableExistsException tableExistsException) {
            System.out.println("Table already exist : " +
tableName);
            if(admin != null) {
                try {
                admin.close();
                } catch (IOException ioException) {
                    System.out.println("Error occure while
closing the HBaseAdmin connection : " + ioException);
                }
            }
        }catch (MasterNotRunningException e) {
            throw new RuntimeException("HBase master not
running, table creation failed : ");
        } catch (ZooKeeperConnectionException e) {
            throw new RuntimeException("Zookeeper not running,
table creation failed : ");
        } catch (IOException e) {
            throw new RuntimeException("IO error, table
creation failed : ");
        }
    }
    /**
     * This method insert the input record into HBase.
     *
     * @param record
     *          input record
```

```
     * @param rowId
     *              unique id to identify each record uniquely.
     */
    public void insert(Map<String, Map<String, Object>> record,
String rowId) {
        try {
        Put put = new Put(Bytes.toBytes(rowId));
        for (String cf : record.keySet()) {
            for (String column: record.get(cf).keySet()) {
                put.add(Bytes.toBytes(cf),
Bytes.toBytes(column),
Bytes.toBytes(record.get(cf).get(column).toString()));
            }
        }
        hTable.put(put);
        }catch (Exception e) {
            throw new RuntimeException("Error occure while
storing record into HBase");
        }
    }

    public static void main(String[] args) {
        List<String> cFs = new ArrayList<String>();
        cFs.add("cf1");
        cFs.add("cf2");

        List<String> zks = new ArrayList<String>();
        zks.add("192.168.41.122");
        Map<String, Map<String, Object>> record = new
HashMap<String, Map<String,Object>>();
        Map<String, Object> cf1 = new HashMap<String,
Object>();
        cf1.put("aa", "1");
        Map<String, Object> cf2 = new HashMap<String,
Object>();
        cf2.put("bb", "1");
        record.put("cf1", cf1);
        record.put("cf2", cf2);
        HBaseOperations hbaseOperations = new
HBaseOperations("tableName", cFs, zks, 2181);
        hbaseOperations.insert(record,
UUID.randomUUID().toString());

    }
}
```

4. Create a `SampleSpout` class in the `com.stormadvance.stormhbase` package. This class generates random records and passes them to the next action (bolt) in the topology. The following is the format of the record generated by the `SampleSpout` class:

```
["john","watson","abc"]
```

The following is the source code of the `SampleSpout` class:

```
public class SampleSpout extends BaseRichSpout {
    private static final long serialVersionUID = 1L;
    private SpoutOutputCollector spoutOutputCollector;
    private static final Map<Integer, String> FIRSTNAMEMAP = new
HashMap<Integer, String>();
    static {
        FIRSTNAMEMAP.put(0, "john");
        FIRSTNAMEMAP.put(1, "nick");
        FIRSTNAMEMAP.put(2, "mick");
        FIRSTNAMEMAP.put(3, "tom");
        FIRSTNAMEMAP.put(4, "jerry");
    }
    private static final Map<Integer, String> LASTNAME = new
HashMap<Integer, String>();
    static {
        LASTNAME.put(0, "anderson");
        LASTNAME.put(1, "watson");
        LASTNAME.put(2, "ponting");
        LASTNAME.put(3, "dravid");
        LASTNAME.put(4, "lara");
    }
    private static final Map<Integer, String> COMPANYNAME = new
HashMap<Integer, String>();
    static {
        COMPANYNAME.put(0, "abc");
        COMPANYNAME.put(1, "dfg");
        COMPANYNAME.put(2, "pqr");
        COMPANYNAME.put(3, "ecd");
        COMPANYNAME.put(4, "awe");
    }

    public void open(Map conf, TopologyContext context,
            SpoutOutputCollector spoutOutputCollector) {
        // Open the spout
        this.spoutOutputCollector = spoutOutputCollector;
    }

    public void nextTuple() {
```

```
        // Storm cluster repeatedly call this method to emit the
continuous //
        // stream of tuples.
        final Random rand = new Random();
        // generate the random number from 0 to 4.
        int randomNumber = rand.nextInt(5);
        spoutOutputCollector.emit (new
Values(FIRSTNAMEMAP.get(randomNumber),LASTNAME.get(randomNumber),CO
MPANYNAME.get(randomNumber)));
    }

    public void declareOutputFields(OutputFieldsDeclarer declarer)
{
        // emits the field  firstName , lastName and companyName.
        declarer.declare(new
Fields("firstName","lastName","companyName"));
    }
}
```

5. Create a `StormHBaseBolt` class in the `com.stormadvance.stormhbase`
   package. This bolt receives the tuples emitted by `SampleSpout` and then calls the
   `insert()` method of the `HBaseOperations` class to insert the record into HBase.
   The following is the source code of the `StormHBaseBolt` class:

```
public class StormHBaseBolt implements IBasicBolt {

    private static final long serialVersionUID = 2L;
    private HBaseOperations hbaseOperations;
    private String tableName;
    private List<String> columnFamilies;
    private List<String> zookeeperIPs;
    private int zkPort;
    /**
     * Constructor of StormHBaseBolt class
     *
     * @param tableName
     *             HBaseTableNam
     * @param columnFamilies
     *             List of column families
     * @param zookeeperIPs
     *             List of zookeeper nodes
     * @param zkPort
     *             Zookeeper client port
     */
    public StormHBaseBolt(String tableName, List<String>
columnFamilies,
            List<String> zookeeperIPs, int zkPort) {
```

```java
            this.tableName =tableName;
            this.columnFamilies = columnFamilies;
            this.zookeeperIPs = zookeeperIPs;
            this.zkPort = zkPort;

    }

    public void execute(Tuple input, BasicOutputCollector
collector) {
            Map<String, Map<String, Object>> record = new
HashMap<String, Map<String, Object>>();
            Map<String, Object> personalMap = new HashMap<String,
Object>();
            // "firstName","lastName","companyName")
            personalMap.put("firstName",
input.getValueByField("firstName"));
            personalMap.put("lastName",
input.getValueByField("lastName"));

            Map<String, Object> companyMap = new HashMap<String,
Object>();
            companyMap.put("companyName",
input.getValueByField("companyName"));

            record.put("personal", personalMap);
            record.put("company", companyMap);
            // call the inset method of HBaseOperations class to insert
record into
            // HBase
            hbaseOperations.insert(record,
UUID.randomUUID().toString());
    }

    public void declareOutputFields(OutputFieldsDeclarer declarer)
{

    }

    public Map<String, Object> getComponentConfiguration() {
        // TODO Auto-generated method stub
        return null;
    }

    public void prepare(Map stormConf, TopologyContext context) {
        // create the instance of HBaseOperations class
        hbaseOperations = new HBaseOperations(tableName,
columnFamilies,
                    zookeeperIPs, zkPort);
```

```
    }

    public void cleanup() {
        // TODO Auto-generated method stub

    }

}
```

The constructor of the `StormHBaseBolt` class takes the HBase table name, column families list, ZooKeeper IP address, and ZooKeeper port as an argument and sets the class level variables. The `prepare()` method of the `StormHBaseBolt` class will create an instance of the `HBaseOperatons` class.

The `execute()` method of the `StormHBaseBolt` class takes an input tuple as an argument and converts it into the HBase structure format. It also uses the `java.util.UUID` class to generate the HBase row ID.

6. Create a `Topology` class in the `com.stormadvance.stormhbase` package. This class creates an instance of the spout and bolt classes and chains them together using a `TopologyBuilder` class. The following is the implementation of the main class:

```
public class Topology {
    public static void main(String[] args) throws
AlreadyAliveException,
            InvalidTopologyException {
        TopologyBuilder builder = new TopologyBuilder();

        List<String> zks = new ArrayList<String>();
        zks.add("127.0.0.1");

        List<String> cFs = new ArrayList<String>();
        cFs.add("personal");
        cFs.add("company");

        // set the spout class
        builder.setSpout("spout", new SampleSpout(), 2);
        // set the bolt class
        builder.setBolt("bolt", new StormHBaseBolt("user", cFs,
zks, 2181), 2)
                .shuffleGrouping("spout");
        Config conf = new Config();
        conf.setDebug(true);
        // create an instance of LocalCluster class for
        // executing topology in local mode.
```

```
            LocalCluster cluster = new LocalCluster();

            // LearningStormTopolgy is the name of submitted topology.
            cluster.submitTopology("StormHBaseTopology", conf,
                    builder.createTopology());
            try {
                Thread.sleep(60000);
            } catch (Exception exception) {
                System.out.println("Thread interrupted exception : " +
        exception);
            }
            System.out.println("Stopped Called : ");
            // kill the LearningStormTopology
            cluster.killTopology("StormHBaseTopology");
            // shutdown the storm test cluster
            cluster.shutdown();


        }
    }
```

In this section, we covered how you can integrate Storm with a NoSQL database, HBase. In the next section, we are going to cover the integration of Storm with Redis.

Integrating Storm with Redis

Redis is a key value data store. The key values can be strings, lists, sets, hashes, and so on. It is extremely fast because the entire dataset is stored in the memory. The following are the steps to install Redis:

1. First, you will need to install make, gcc, and cc to compile the Redis code using the following command:

```
sudo yum -y install make gcc cc
```

2. Download, unpack, and make Redis, and copy it to `/usr/local/bin` using the following commands:

```
cd /home/$USER
Here, $USER is the name of the Linux user.
http://download.redis.io/releases/redis-2.6.16.tar.gz
tar -xvf redis-2.6.16.tar.gz
cd redis-2.6.16
make
sudo cp src/redis-server /usr/local/bin
sudo cp src/redis-cli /usr/local/bin
```

3. Execute the following commands to make Redis a service:

```
sudo mkdir -p /etc/redis
sudo mkdir -p /var/redis
cd /home/$USER/redis-2.6.16/
sudo cp utils/redis_init_script /etc/init.d/redis
wget https://bitbucket.org/ptylr/public-stuff/raw/41d5c8e87ce6adb3
4aa16cd571c3f04fb4d5e7ac/etc/init.d/redis
sudo cp redis /etc/init.d/redis
cd /home/$USER/redis-2.6.16/
sudo cp redis.conf /etc/redis/redis.conf
```

4. Now, run the following commands to add the service to `chkconfig`, set it to autostart, and actually start the service:

```
chkconfig --add redis
chkconfig redis on
service redis start
```

5. Check the installation of Redis with the following command:

```
redis-cli ping
```

If the result of the test command is PONG, then the installation has been successful.

We will assume that you have the Redis service up and running.

Next, we will create a sample Storm topology that will explain how you can store the data processed by Storm in Redis.

6. Create a Maven project using `com.stormadvance` for the `groupID` and `stormredis` for the `artifactID`.

7. Add the following dependencies and repositories in the `pom.xml` file:

```xml
<repositories>
        <repository>
            <id>central</id>
            <name>Maven Central</name>
            <url>http://repo1.maven.org/maven2/</url>
        </repository>
        <repository>
            <id>cloudera-repo</id>
            <name>Cloudera CDH</name>
<url>https://repository.cloudera.com/artifactory/cloudera-
            repos/</url>
        </repository>
        <repository>
            <id>clojars.org</id>
            <url>http://clojars.org/repo</url>
        </repository>
    </repositories>
    <dependencies>
        <dependency>
            <groupId>storm</groupId>
            <artifactId>storm</artifactId>
            <version>0.9.0.1</version>
        </dependency>
                <dependency>
            <groupId>com.fasterxml.jackson.core</groupId>
            <artifactId>jackson-core</artifactId>
            <version>2.1.1</version>
        </dependency>

        <dependency>
            <groupId>com.fasterxml.jackson.core</groupId>
            <artifactId>jackson-databind</artifactId>
            <version>2.1.1</version>
        </dependency>
        <dependency>
            <groupId>junit</groupId>
            <artifactId>junit</artifactId>
            <version>3.8.1</version>
            <scope>test</scope>
        </dependency>
        <dependency>
            <groupId>redis.clients</groupId>
            <artifactId>jedis</artifactId>
            <version>2.4.2</version>
        </dependency>
    </dependencies>
```

8. Create a `RedisOperations` class in the `com.stormadvance.stormredis` package. The `RedisOperations` class contains the following method:
   - `insert(Map<String, Object> record, String id)`: This method takes the record and ID as input and inserts the input record in Redis. In the `insert()` method, we will first serialize the record into a string using the Jackson library and then store the serialized record into Redis. Each record must have a unique ID because it is used to retrieve the record from Redis.

The following is the source code of the `RedisOperations` class:

```
public class RedisOperations implements Serializable {


    private static final long serialVersionUID = 1L;
    Jedis jedis = null;

    public RedisOperations(String redisIP, int port) {
        // Connecting to Redis on localhost
        jedis = new Jedis(redisIP, port);
    }

    public void insert(Map<String, Object> record, String id) {
        try {
            jedis.set(id, new
ObjectMapper().writeValueAsString(record));
        } catch (Exception e) {
            System.out.println("Record not persist into datastore :
");
        }
    }
}
```

We will use the same `SampleSpout` class created in the *Integrating Storm with HBase* section.

9. Create a `StormRedisBolt` class in the `com.stormadvance.stormredis` package. This bolt receives the tuples emitted by the `SampleSpout` class, converts them to the Redis structure, and then calls the `insert()` method of the `RedisOperations` class to insert the record into Redis. The following is the source code of the `StormRedisBolt` class:

```
public class StormRedisBolt implements IBasicBolt{
private static final long serialVersionUID = 2L;
private RedisOperations redisOperations = null;
```

```
        private String redisIP = null;
        private int port;
        public StormRedisBolt(String redisIP, int port) {
            this.redisIP = redisIP;
            this.port = port;
        }
        public void execute(Tuple input, BasicOutputCollector
collector) {
            Map<String, Object> record = new HashMap<String, Object>();
            //"firstName","lastName","companyName")
            record.put("firstName",
input.getValueByField("firstName"));
            record.put("lastName", input.getValueByField("lastName"));
            record.put("companyName",
input.getValueByField("companyName"));
            redisOperations.insert(record,
UUID.randomUUID().toString());
        }

        public void declareOutputFields(OutputFieldsDeclarer declarer)
{
        }

        public Map<String, Object> getComponentConfiguration() {
            return null;
        }

        public void prepare(Map stormConf, TopologyContext context) {
            redisOperations = new RedisOperations(this.redisIP,
this.port);
        }

        public void cleanup() {
        }

    }
```

In the `StormRedisBolt` class, we use the `java.util.UUID` class to generate the Redis key.

10. Create a `Topology` class in the `com.stormadvance.stormredis` package. This class creates an instance of the `spout` and `bolt` classes and chains them together using a `TopologyBuilder` class. The following is the implementation of the main class:

```
public class Topology {
    public static void main(String[] args) throws
```

```
        AlreadyAliveException,
                InvalidTopologyException {
        TopologyBuilder builder = new TopologyBuilder();
        List<String> zks = new ArrayList<String>();
        zks.add("192.168.41.122");
        List<String> cFs = new ArrayList<String>();
        cFs.add("personal");
        cFs.add("company");
        // set the spout class
        builder.setSpout("spout", new SampleSpout(), 2);
        // set the bolt class
        builder.setBolt("bolt", new
StormRedisBolt("192.168.41.122",2181), 2).shuffleGrouping("spout");

        Config conf = new Config();
        conf.setDebug(true);
        // create an instance of LocalCluster class for
        // executing topology in local mode.
        LocalCluster cluster = new LocalCluster();

        // LearningStormTopolgy is the name of submitted topology.
        cluster.submitTopology("StormRedisTopology", conf,
                builder.createTopology());
        try {
            Thread.sleep(10000);
        } catch (Exception exception) {
            System.out.println("Thread interrupted exception : " +
exception);
        }
        // kill the LearningStormTopology
        cluster.killTopology("StormRedisTopology");
        // shutdown the storm test cluster
        cluster.shutdown();
    }
}
```

In this section, we covered the installation of Redis and how we can integrate Storm with Redis.

Integrating Storm with Elasticsearch

In this section, we are going to cover the installation of Storm with Elasticsearch. Elasticsearch is an open source, distributed search engine platform developed on Lucene. It provides a multitenant-capable, full-text search engine capability.

We are assuming that Elasticsearch is running on your environment. Please refer to `https://www.elastic.co/guide/en/elasticsearch/reference/2.3/_installation.html` to install Elasticsearch on any of the boxes if you don't have any running Elasticsearch cluster. Go through the following steps to integrate Storm with Elasticsearch:

1. Create a Maven project using `com.stormadvance` for the `groupID` and `storm_elasticsearch` for the `artifactID`.

2. Add the following dependencies and repositories to the `pom.xml` file:

```
<dependencies>
        <dependency>
            <groupId>org.elasticsearch</groupId>
            <artifactId>elasticsearch</artifactId>
            <version>2.4.4</version>
        </dependency>
        <dependency>
            <groupId>junit</groupId>
            <artifactId>junit</artifactId>
            <version>3.8.1</version>
            <scope>test</scope>
        </dependency>
        <dependency>
            <groupId>org.apache.storm</groupId>
            <artifactId>storm-core</artifactId>
            <version>1.0.2</version>
            <scope>provided</scope>
        </dependency>
</dependencies>
```

3. Create an `ElasticSearchOperation` class in the `com.stormadvance.storm_elasticsearch` package. The `ElasticSearchOperation` class contains the following method:

   - `insert(Map<String, Object> data, String indexName, String indexMapping, String indexId)`: This method takes the record data, `indexName`, `indexMapping`, and `indexId` as input, and inserts the input record in Elasticsearch.

   The following is the source code of the `ElasticSearchOperation` class:

```
public class ElasticSearchOperation {

    private TransportClient client;

    public ElasticSearchOperation(List<String> esNodes) throws
Exception {
```

```
        try {
            Settings settings = Settings.settingsBuilder()
                    .put("cluster.name", "elasticsearch").build();
            client =
TransportClient.builder().settings(settings).build();
            for (String esNode : esNodes) {
                client.addTransportAddress(new
InetSocketTransportAddress(
                        InetAddress.getByName(esNode), 9300));
            }

        } catch (Exception e) {
            throw e;
        }

    }

    public void insert(Map<String, Object> data, String indexName,
String indexMapping, String indexId) {
        client.prepareIndex(indexName, indexMapping, indexId)
                .setSource(data).get();
    }
    public static void main(String[] s){
        try{
            List<String> esNodes = new ArrayList<String>();
            esNodes.add("127.0.0.1");
            ElasticSearchOperation elasticSearchOperation  = new
ElasticSearchOperation(esNodes);
            Map<String, Object> data = new HashMap<String,
Object>();
            data.put("name", "name");
            data.put("add", "add");
elasticSearchOperation.insert(data,"indexName","indexMapping",UUID.
randomUUID().toString());
        }catch(Exception e) {
            e.printStackTrace();
            //System.out.println(e);
        }
    }
}
```

We will use the same `SampleSpout` class created in the *Integrating Storm with HBase* section.

4. Create an `ESBolt` class in the `com.stormadvance.storm_elasticsearch` package. This bolt receives the tuples emitted by the `SampleSpout` class, converts it to the `Map` structure, and then calls the `insert()` method of the `ElasticSearchOperation` class to insert the record into Elasticsearch. The following is the source code of the `ESBolt` class:

```
public class ESBolt implements IBasicBolt {

    private static final long serialVersionUID = 2L;
    private ElasticSearchOperation elasticSearchOperation;
    private List<String> esNodes;

    /**
     *
     * @param esNodes
     */
    public ESBolt(List<String> esNodes) {
        this.esNodes = esNodes;

    }

    public void execute(Tuple input, BasicOutputCollector
collector) {
        Map<String, Object> personalMap = new HashMap<String,
Object>();
        // "firstName","lastName","companyName")
        personalMap.put("firstName",
input.getValueByField("firstName"));
        personalMap.put("lastName",
input.getValueByField("lastName"));

        personalMap.put("companyName",
input.getValueByField("companyName"));
elasticSearchOperation.insert(personalMap,"person","personmapping",
UUID.randomUUID().toString());
    }

    public void declareOutputFields(OutputFieldsDeclarer declarer)
{

    }

    public Map<String, Object> getComponentConfiguration() {
        // TODO Auto-generated method stub
        return null;
    }
```

```
        public void prepare(Map stormConf, TopologyContext context) {
            try {
                // create the instance of ESOperations class
                elasticSearchOperation = new
    ElasticSearchOperation(esNodes);
            } catch (Exception e) {
                throw new RuntimeException();
            }
        }

        public void cleanup() {

        }

    }
```

5. Create an `ESTopology` class in the `com.stormadvance.storm_elasticsearch` package. This class creates an instance of the `spout` and `bolt` classes and chains them together using a `TopologyBuilder` class. The following is the implementation of the main class:

```
    public class ESTopology {
        public static void main(String[] args) throws
    AlreadyAliveException,
                InvalidTopologyException {
            TopologyBuilder builder = new TopologyBuilder();

            //ES Node list
            List<String> esNodes = new ArrayList<String>();
            esNodes.add("10.191.209.14");

            // set the spout class
            builder.setSpout("spout", new SampleSpout(), 2);
            // set the ES bolt class
            builder.setBolt("bolt", new ESBolt(esNodes), 2)
                    .shuffleGrouping("spout");
            Config conf = new Config();
            conf.setDebug(true);
            // create an instance of LocalCluster class for
            // executing topology in local mode.
            LocalCluster cluster = new LocalCluster();

            // ESTopology is the name of submitted topology.
            cluster.submitTopology("ESTopology", conf,
                    builder.createTopology());
            try {
                Thread.sleep(60000);
```

```
        } catch (Exception exception) {
            System.out.println("Thread interrupted exception : " +
exception);
        }
        System.out.println("Stopped Called : ");
        // kill the LearningStormTopology
        cluster.killTopology("StormHBaseTopology");
        // shutdown the storm test cluster
        cluster.shutdown();


    }
}
```

In this section, we covered how we can store the data into Elasticsearch by making the connection with Elasticsearch nodes inside the Storm bolts.

Integrating Storm with Esper

In this section, we are going to cover how we can use the windowing operation inside Storm by using Esper. Esper is an open source event series analysis and event correlation engine for **complex event processing** (**CEP**).

Please refer to `http://www.espertech.com/products/esper.php` to read more details about Esper. Go through the following steps to integrate Storm with Esper:

1. Create a Maven project using `com.stormadvance` for the `groupID` and `storm_esper` for the `artifactID`.
2. Add the following dependencies and repositories in the `pom.xml` file:

```
<dependencies>
    <dependency>
        <groupId>com.espertech</groupId>
        <artifactId>esper</artifactId>
        <version>5.3.0</version>
    </dependency>
    <dependency>
        <groupId>junit</groupId>
        <artifactId>junit</artifactId>
        <version>3.8.1</version>
        <scope>test</scope>
    </dependency>
    <dependency>
        <groupId>org.apache.storm</groupId>
        <artifactId>storm-core</artifactId>
```

```
                <version>1.0.2</version>
                <scope>provided</scope>
            </dependency>
        </dependencies>
```

3. Create an `EsperOperation` class in the
   `com.stormadvance.storm_elasticsearch` package. The `EsperOperation`
   class contains the following method:
   - `esperPut(Stock stock)`: This method takes the stock bean as an
     input and sends the event to the Esper listener.

The constructor of the `EsperOperation` class initializes the Esper listener and
sets the Esper query. The Esper query buffers the events over 5 minutes and
returns the total sales of each product during the 5 minutes window. Here, we are
using the fixed batch window.

The following is the source code of the `EsperOperation` class:

```
public class EsperOperation {

    private EPRuntime cepRT = null;

    public EsperOperation() {
        Configuration cepConfig = new Configuration();
        cepConfig.addEventType("StockTick", Stock.class.getName());
        EPServiceProvider cep =
EPServiceProviderManager.getProvider(
                "myCEPEngine", cepConfig);
        cepRT = cep.getEPRuntime();

        EPAdministrator cepAdm = cep.getEPAdministrator();
        EPStatement cepStatement = cepAdm
                .createEPL("select sum(price),product from "
                    + "StockTick.win:time_batch(5 sec) "
                    + "group by product");

        cepStatement.addListener(new CEPListener());
    }

    public static class CEPListener implements UpdateListener {

        public void update(EventBean[] newData, EventBean[]
oldData) {
            try {
                System.out.println("################### Event
received:
```

```
                        "+newData);
                        for (EventBean eventBean : newData) {
                            System.out.println("************************
Event
                              received 1: " + eventBean.getUnderlying());
                        }
                } catch (Exception e) {
                    e.printStackTrace();
                    System.out.println(e);
                }
            }
        }

    public void esperPut(Stock stock) {
        cepRT.sendEvent(stock);
    }

    private static Random generator = new Random();

    public static void main(String[] s) throws InterruptedException
{
        EsperOperation esperOperation = new EsperOperation();
        // We generate a few ticks...
        for (int i = 0; i < 5; i++) {
            double price = (double) generator.nextInt(10);
            long timeStamp = System.currentTimeMillis();
            String product = "AAPL";
            Stock stock = new Stock(product, price, timeStamp);
            System.out.println("Sending tick:" + stock);
            esperOperation.esperPut(stock);
        }
        Thread.sleep(200000);
    }

}
```

4. Create a `SampleSpout` class in the `com.stormadvance.storm_esper` package. This class generates random records and passes them to the next action (bolt) in the topology. The following is the format of the record generated by the `SampleSpout` class:

```
["product type","price","sale date"]
```

The following is the source code of the `SampleSpout` class:

```
public class SampleSpout extends BaseRichSpout {
    private static final long serialVersionUID = 1L;
    private SpoutOutputCollector spoutOutputCollector;
    private static final Map<Integer, String> PRODUCT = new
    HashMap<Integer, String>();
    static {
        PRODUCT.put(0, "A");
        PRODUCT.put(1, "B");
        PRODUCT.put(2, "C");
        PRODUCT.put(3, "D");
        PRODUCT.put(4, "E");
    }
    private static final Map<Integer, Double> price = new
    HashMap<Integer, Double>();
    static {
        price.put(0, 500.0);
        price.put(1, 100.0);
        price.put(2, 300.0);
        price.put(3, 900.0);
        price.put(4, 1000.0);
    }
    public void open(Map conf, TopologyContext context,
            SpoutOutputCollector spoutOutputCollector) {
        // Open the spout
        this.spoutOutputCollector = spoutOutputCollector;
    }

    public void nextTuple() {
        // Storm cluster repeatedly call this method to emit the
        continuous //
        // stream of tuples.
        final Random rand = new Random();
        // generate the random number from 0 to 4.
        int randomNumber = rand.nextInt(5);
        spoutOutputCollector.emit(new
        Values(PRODUCT.get(randomNumber),price.get(randomNumber),
        System.currentTimeMillis()));
        try {
```

```
                  Thread.sleep(1000);
            } catch (InterruptedException e) {
                // TODO Auto-generated catch block
                e.printStackTrace();
            }
        }

    public void declareOutputFields(OutputFieldsDeclarer declarer)
    {
            // emits the field  firstName , lastName and companyName.
            declarer.declare(new
    Fields("product","price","timestamp"));
        }
    }
```

5. Create an `EsperBolt` class in the `com.stormadvance.storm_esper` package. This bolt receives the tuples emitted by the `SampleSpout` class, converts it to the stock bean, and then calls the `esperPut()` method of the `EsperBolt` class to pass the data to the Esper engine. The following is the source code of the `EsperBolt` class:

```
public class EsperBolt implements IBasicBolt {

    private static final long serialVersionUID = 2L;
    private EsperOperation esperOperation;

    public EsperBolt() {

    }

    public void execute(Tuple input, BasicOutputCollector
    collector) {
            double price = input.getDoubleByField("price");
            long timeStamp = input.getLongByField("timestamp");
            //long timeStamp = System.currentTimeMillis();
            String product = input.getStringByField("product");
            Stock stock = new Stock(product, price, timeStamp);
            esperOperation.esperPut(stock);
        }

    public void declareOutputFields(OutputFieldsDeclarer declarer)
    {

        }

    public Map<String, Object> getComponentConfiguration() {
            // TODO Auto-generated method stub
```

```
            return null;
        }

    public void prepare(Map stormConf, TopologyContext context) {
        try {
            // create the instance of ESOperations class
            esperOperation = new EsperOperation();
        } catch (Exception e) {
            throw new RuntimeException();
        }
    }

    public void cleanup() {

    }
}
```

6. Create an `EsperTopology` class in the `com.stormadvance.storm_esper` package. This class creates an instance of the `spout` and `bolt` classes and chains them together using a `TopologyBuilder` class. The following is the implementation of the main class:

```
public class EsperTopology {
    public static void main(String[] args) throws
AlreadyAliveException,
            InvalidTopologyException {
        TopologyBuilder builder = new TopologyBuilder();

        // set the spout class
        builder.setSpout("spout", new SampleSpout(), 2);
        // set the ES bolt class
        builder.setBolt("bolt", new EsperBolt(), 2)
                .shuffleGrouping("spout");
        Config conf = new Config();
        conf.setDebug(true);
        // create an instance of LocalCluster class for
        // executing topology in local mode.
        LocalCluster cluster = new LocalCluster();

        // EsperTopology is the name of submitted topology.
        cluster.submitTopology("EsperTopology", conf,
                builder.createTopology());
        try {
            Thread.sleep(60000);
        } catch (Exception exception) {
            System.out.println("Thread interrupted exception : " +
exception);
```

```
                    }
                    System.out.println("Stopped Called : ");
                    // kill the LearningStormTopology
                    cluster.killTopology("EsperTopology");
                    // shutdown the storm test cluster
                    cluster.shutdown();

            }
        }
```

Summary

In this chapter, we mostly focused on the integration of Storm with other databases. Also, we covered how we can use Esper inside Storm to perform the windowing operation.

In the next chapter, we will cover the Apache log processing case study. We will explain how you can generate business information by processing log files through Storm.

11
Apache Log Processing with Storm

In the previous chapter, we covered how we can integrate Storm with Redis, HBase, Esper and Elasticsearch.

In this chapter, we are covering the most popular use case of Storm, which is log processing.

This chapter covers the following major sections:

- Apache log processing elements
- Installation of Logstash
- Configuring Logstash to produce the Apache log into Kafka
- Splitting the Apache log file
- Calculating the country name, operating system type, and browser type
- Identifying the search key words of your website
- Persisting the process data
- Kafka spout and defining the topology
- Deploying the topology
- Storing the data into Elasticsearch and reporting

Apache log processing elements

Log processing is becoming a necessity for every organization, as they need to collect the business information from log data. In this chapter, we are basically working on how we can process the Apache log data using Logstash, Kafka, Storm, and Elasticsearch to collect the business information.

The following diagram illustrates all the elements that we are developing in this chapter:

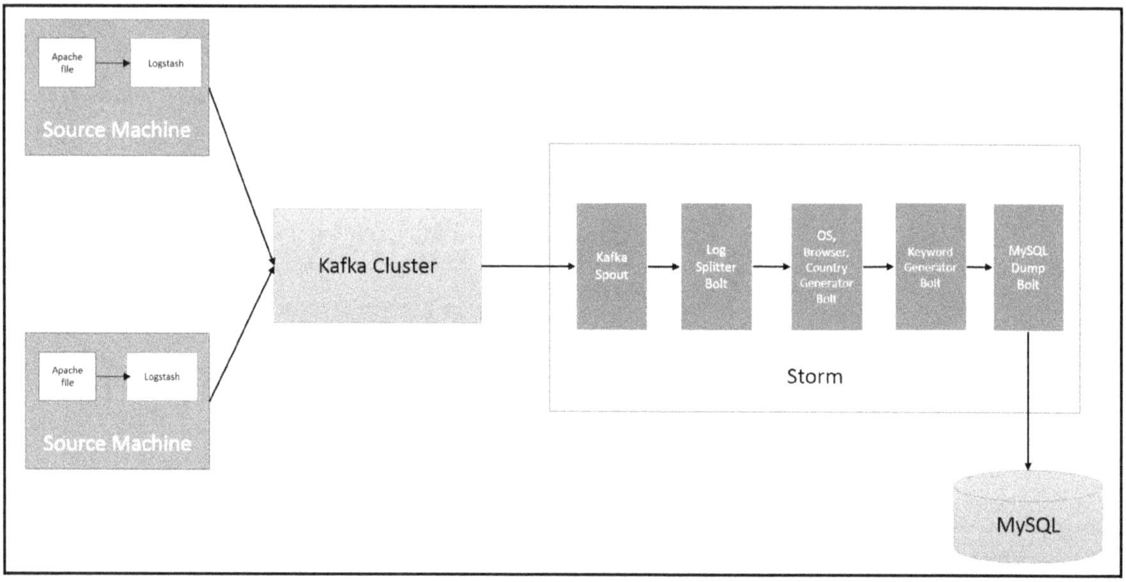

Figure 11.1: Log processing topology

Producing Apache log in Kafka using Logstash

As explained in Chapter 8, *Integration of Storm and Kafka*, Kafka is a distributed messaging queue and can integrate very well with Storm. In this section, we will show you how we can use Logstash to read the Apache log file and publish it into the Kafka Cluster. We are assuming you already have the Kafka Cluster running. The installation steps of the Kafka Cluster are outlined in Chapter 8, *Integration of Storm and Kafka*.

Installation of Logstash

Before moving on to the installation of Logstash, we are going to answer the questions: What is Logstash? Why are we using Logstash?

What is Logstash?

Logstash is a tool that is used to collect, filter/parse, and emit the data for future use. Collect, parse, and emit are divided into three sections, which are called input, filter, and output:

- The **input** section is used to read the data from external sources. The common input sources are File, TCP port, Kafka, and so on.
- The **filter** section is used to parse the data.
- The **output** section is used to emit the data to some external source. The common external sources are Kafka, Elasticsearch, TCP, and so on.

Why are we using Logstash?

We need to read the log data in real time and store it into Kafka before Storm starts the actual processing. We are using Logstash as it is very mature in reading the log files and pushing the logs data into Kafka.

Installation of Logstash

We should have JDK 1.8 installed on the Linux box before installing Logstash, as we are going to use Logstash 5.4.1 and JDK 1.8 is the minimum requirement for this. The following are the steps to install Logstash:

1. Download Logstash 5.4.1 from `https://artifacts.elastic.co/downloads/logstash/logstash-5.4.1.zip`.
2. Copy the setup on all the machines whose Apache logs you want to publish into Kafka.
3. Extract the setup by running the following command:

```
> unzip logstash-5.4.1.zip
```

Configuration of Logstash

Now, we are going to define the Logstash configuration to consume the Apache logs and store them into Kafka.

Create a `logstash.conf` file and add the following lines:

```
input {
  file {
    path => "PATH_TO_APACHE_LOG"
    start_position => "beginning"
  }
}
output {
  kafka {
    topic_id => "TOPIC_NAME"
    bootstrap_servers => "KAFKA_IP:KAFKA_PORT"
  }
}
```

We should change the following parameters in the preceding configuration:

- `TOPIC_NAME`: Replace with the Kafka topic you want to use for storing the Apache log
- `KAFKA_IP` and `KAFKA_PORT`: Specify the comma separated list of all the Kafka nodes
- `PATH_TO_APACHE_LOG`: The location of Apache log file on the Logstash machine

Go to Logstash home directory and execute the following command to start the log reading and publishing into Kafka:

```
$ bin/logstash agent -f logstash.conf
```

Now, the real-time log data is coming into the Kafka topic. In the next section, we are writing the Storm topology to consume the log data, process, and store the process data into the database.

Why are we using Kafka between Logstash and Storm?

As we all know, Storm provides guaranteed message processing, meaning that every message enters into the Storm topology and will be processed at least once. In Storm, data loss is possible only at the spout end, if the processing capacity of Storm spout is less than the producing capacity of Logstash. Hence, to avoid the data getting lost at the Storm spout end, we will generally publish the data into a messaging queue (Kafka) and Storm spout will use the messaging queue as the data source.

Splitting the Apache log line

Now, we are creating a new topology, which will read the data from Kafka using the KafkaSpout spout. In this section, we are writing an ApacheLogSplitter bolt, that has a logic to fetch the IP, status code, referrer, bytes sent, and so on, information from the Apache log line. As this is a new topology, we must first create the new project.

1. Create a new Maven project with groupId as com.stormadvance and artifactId as logprocessing.

2. Add the following dependencies in the pom.xml file:

```
<dependency>
        <groupId>org.apache.storm</groupId>
        <artifactId>storm-core</artifactId>
        <version>1.0.2</version>
        <scope>provided</scope>
</dependency>

<!-- Utilities -->
<dependency>
        <groupId>commons-collections</groupId>
        <artifactId>commons-collections</artifactId>
        <version>3.2.1</version>
</dependency>
<dependency>
        <groupId>com.google.guava</groupId>
        <artifactId>guava</artifactId>
        <version>15.0</version>
</dependency>
```

3. We are creating an ApacheLogSplitter class in the com.stormadvance.logprocessing package. This class contains logic to fetch the different elements such as IP, referrer, user-agent, and so on, from the Apache log line.

```
/**
 * This class contains logic to Parse an Apache log file with Regular
 * Expressions
 */
public class ApacheLogSplitter {
 public Map<String,Object> logSplitter(String apacheLog) {
        String logEntryLine = apacheLog;
        // Regex pattern to split fetch the different properties
from log lines.
```

```
                    String logEntryPattern = "^([\\d.]+) (\\S+) (\\S+) \\[([\\w-
    :/]+\\s[+\\-]\\d{4})\\] \"(.+?)\" (\\d{3}) (\\d+) \"([^\"]+)\"
    \"([^\"]+)\"";

            Pattern p = Pattern.compile(logEntryPattern);
            Matcher matcher = p.matcher(logEntryLine);
            Map<String,Object> logMap = new HashMap<String, Object>();
            if (!matcher.matches() || 9 != matcher.groupCount()) {
                    System.err.println("Bad log entry (or problem with
    RE?):");
                    System.err.println(logEntryLine);
                    return logMap;
            }
            // set the ip, dateTime, request, etc into map.
            logMap.put("ip", matcher.group(1));
            logMap.put("dateTime", matcher.group(4));
            logMap.put("request", matcher.group(5));
            logMap.put("response", matcher.group(6));
            logMap.put("bytesSent", matcher.group(7));
            logMap.put("referrer", matcher.group(8));
            logMap.put("useragent", matcher.group(9));
            return logMap;
    }
```

4. The input for the `logSplitter(String apacheLog)` method is:

```
98.83.179.51 - - [18/May/2011:19:35:08 -0700] \"GET /css/main.css
HTTP/1.1\" 200 1837 \"http://www.safesand.com/information.htm\"
\"Mozilla/5.0 (Windows NT 6.0; WOW64; rv:2.0.1) Gecko/20100101
Firefox/4.0.1\"
```

5. The output of the `logSplitter(String apacheLog)` method is:

```
{response=200, referrer=http://www.safesand.com/information.htm,
bytesSent=1837, useragent=Mozilla/5.0 (Windows NT 6.0; WOW64;
rv:2.0.1) Gecko/20100101 Firefox/4.0.1,
dateTime=18/May/2011:19:35:08 -0700, request=GET /css/main.css
HTTP/1.1, ip=98.83.179.51}
```

6. Now we will create the `ApacheLogSplitterBolt` class in the
   `com.stormadvance.logprocessing` package. The `ApacheLogSplitterBolt`
   extends the `org.apache.storm.topology.base.BaseBasicBolt` class and
   passes the set of fields generated by `ApacheLogSplitter` class to the next bolt in
   the topology. The following is the source code of the `ApacheLogSplitterBolt`
   class:

```
/**
 *
 * This class call the ApacheLogSplitter class and pass the set of
fields (ip,
 * referrer, user-agent, etc) to next bolt in Topology.
 */

public class ApacheLogSplitterBolt extends BaseBasicBolt {

 private static final long serialVersionUID = 1L;
 // Create the instance of ApacheLogSplitter class.
 private static final ApacheLogSplitter apacheLogSplitter = new
ApacheLogSplitter();
 private static final List<String> LOG_ELEMENTS = new
ArrayList<String>();
 static {
       LOG_ELEMENTS.add("ip");
       LOG_ELEMENTS.add("dateTime");
       LOG_ELEMENTS.add("request");
       LOG_ELEMENTS.add("response");
       LOG_ELEMENTS.add("bytesSent");
       LOG_ELEMENTS.add("referrer");
       LOG_ELEMENTS.add("useragent");
 }

 public void execute(Tuple input, BasicOutputCollector collector) {
       // Get the Apache log from the tuple
       String log = input.getString(0);

       if (StringUtils.isBlank(log)) {
             // ignore blank lines
             return;
       }
       // call the logSplitter(String apachelog) method of
ApacheLogSplitter
       // class.
       Map<String, Object> logMap =
apacheLogSplitter.logSplitter(log);
       List<Object> logdata = new ArrayList<Object>();
       for (String element : LOG_ELEMENTS) {
```

```
                logdata.add(logMap.get(element));
        }
        // emits set of fields (ip, referrer, user-agent, bytesSent,
etc)
        collector.emit(logdata);

    }

    public void declareOutputFields(OutputFieldsDeclarer declarer) {
        // specify the name of output fields.
        declarer.declare(new Fields("ip", "dateTime", "request",
"response",
                "bytesSent", "referrer", "useragent"));
    }
}
```

The output of the `ApacheLogSplitterBolt` class contains seven fields. These fields are `ip`, `dateTime`, `request`, `response`, `bytesSent`, `referrer`, and `useragent`.

Identifying country, operating system type, and browser type from the log file

This section explains how we can calculate the user country name, operation system type, and browser type by analyzing the Apache log line. By identifying the country name, we can easily identify the location where our site is getting more attention and the location where we are getting less attention. Let's perform the following steps to calculate the country name, operating system, and browser from the Apache log file:

1. We are using the open source `geoip` library to calculate the country name from the IP address. Add the following dependencies in the `pom.xml` file:

   ```xml
   <dependency>
       <groupId>org.geomind</groupId>
       <artifactId>geoip</artifactId>
       <version>1.2.8</version>
   </dependency>
   ```

2. Add the following repository into the `pom.xml` file:

   ```xml
   <repository>
       <id>geoip</id>
       <url>http://snambi.github.com/maven/</url>
   </repository>
   ```

3. We are creating an `IpToCountryConverter` class in the
   `com.stormadvance.logprocessing` package. This class contains the
   parameterized constructor that is taking the location of the `GeoLiteCity.dat`
   file as input. You can find the `GeoLiteCity.dat` file in the resources folder of
   the `logprocessing` project. The location of the `GeoLiteCity.dat` file must be
   the same in all Storm nodes. The `GeoLiteCity.dat` file is a database which we
   are using to calculate the country name from the IP address. The following is the
   source code of the `IpToCountryConverter` class:

```
/**
 * This class contains logic to calculate the country name from IP
address
 *
 */
public class IpToCountryConverter {

 private static LookupService cl = null;

 /**
  * An parameterised constructor which would take the location of
  * GeoLiteCity.dat file as input.
  *
  * @param pathTOGeoLiteCityFile
  */
 public IpToCountryConverter(String pathTOGeoLiteCityFile) {
      try {
            cl = new LookupService("pathTOGeoLiteCityFile",
                      LookupService.GEOIP_MEMORY_CACHE);
      } catch (Exception exception) {
            throw new RuntimeException(
                      "Error occurs while initializing
IpToCountryConverter class : ");
      }
 }

 /**
  * This method takes ip address an input and convert it into
country name.
  *
  * @param ip
  * @return
  */
 public String ipToCountry (String ip) {
      Location location = cl.getLocation(ip);
      if (location == null) {
            return "NA";
```

```
            }
            if (location.countryName == null) {
                return "NA";
            }
            return location.countryName;
        }
    }
```

4. Now download the `UserAgentTools` class from
   `https://code.google.com/p/ndt/source/browse/branches/applet_91/Applet/`
   `src/main/java/edu/internet2/ndt/UserAgentTools.java?r=856`. This class
   contains logic to calculate the operating system and browser type from the user
   agent. You can also find the `UserAgentTools` class in the `logprocessing`
   project.

5. Let's write the `UserInformationGetterBolt` class in the
   `com.stormadvance.logprocessing` package. This bolt uses the
   `UserAgentTools` and `IpToCountryConverter` class to calculate the country
   name, operating system, and browser.

```
/**
 * This class use the IpToCountryConverter and UserAgentTools class
to calculate
 * the country, os and browser from log line.
 *
 */
public class UserInformationGetterBolt extends BaseRichBolt {

    private static final long serialVersionUID = 1L;
    private IpToCountryConverter ipToCountryConverter = null;
    private UserAgentTools userAgentTools = null;
    public OutputCollector collector;
    private String pathTOGeoLiteCityFile;

    public UserInformationGetterBolt(String pathTOGeoLiteCityFile) {
        // set the path of GeoLiteCity.dat file.
        this.pathTOGeoLiteCityFile = pathTOGeoLiteCityFile;
    }

    public void declareOutputFields(OutputFieldsDeclarer declarer) {
        declarer.declare(new Fields("ip", "dateTime", "request",
"response",
                "bytesSent", "referrer", "useragent", "country",
"browser",
                "os"));
    }
```

```
    public void prepare(Map stormConf, TopologyContext context,
            OutputCollector collector) {
        this.collector = collector;
        this.ipToCountryConverter = new IpToCountryConverter(
                this.pathTOGeoLiteCityFile);
        this.userAgentTools = new UserAgentTools();


    }

    public void execute(Tuple input) {

        String ip = input.getStringByField("ip").toString();
        // calculate the country from ip
        Object country = ipToCountryConverter.ipToCountry(ip);
        // calculate the browser from useragent.
        Object browser =
userAgentTools.getBrowser(input.getStringByField(
                "useragent").toString())[1];
        // calculate the os from useragent.
        Object os =
userAgentTools.getOS(input.getStringByField("useragent")
                .toString())[1];
        collector.emit(new Values(input.getString(0),
input.getString(1), input
                .getString(2), input.getString(3),
input.getString(4), input
                .getString(5), input.getString(6), country,
browser, os));

    }
}
```

6. The output of the `UserInformationGetterBolt` class contains 10 fields. These fields are `ip`, `dateTime`, `request`, `response`, `bytesSent`, `referrer`, `useragent`, `country`, `browser`, and `os`.

Calculate the search keyword

This section explains how we can calculate the search keyword from the referrer URL. Suppose a referrer URL is `https://www.google.co.in/#q=learning+storm`. We will pass this referrer URL to a class and the output of the class will be *learning storm*. By identifying the search keyword, we can easily identify the keywords users are searching to reach our site. Let's perform the following steps to calculate the keywords from the referrer URL:

1. We are creating a `KeywordGenerator` class in the `com.stormadvance.logprocessing` package. This class contains logic to generate the search keyword from the referrer URL. The following is the source code of the `KeywordGenerator` class:

```
/**
 * This class takes referrer URL as input, analyze the URL and
return search
 * keyword as output.
 *
 */
public class KeywordGenerator {
 public String getKeyword(String referer) {

        String[] temp;
        Pattern pat = Pattern.compile("[?&#]q=([^&]+)");
        Matcher m = pat.matcher(referer);
        if (m.find()) {
            String searchTerm = null;
            searchTerm = m.group(1);
            temp = searchTerm.split("\\+");
            searchTerm = temp[0];
            for (int i = 1; i < temp.length; i++) {
                searchTerm = searchTerm + " " + temp[i];
            }
            return searchTerm;
        } else {
            pat = Pattern.compile("[?&#]p=([^&]+)");
            m = pat.matcher(referer);
            if (m.find()) {
                String searchTerm = null;
                searchTerm = m.group(1);
                temp = searchTerm.split("\\+");
                searchTerm = temp[0];
                for (int i = 1; i < temp.length; i++) {
                    searchTerm = searchTerm + " " + temp[i];
                }
                return searchTerm;
```

```
                        } else {
                            //
                            pat = Pattern.compile("[?&#]query=([^&]+)");
                            m = pat.matcher(referer);
                            if (m.find()) {
                                String searchTerm = null;
                                searchTerm = m.group(1);
                                temp = searchTerm.split("\\+");
                                searchTerm = temp[0];
                                for (int i = 1; i < temp.length; i++) {
                                    searchTerm = searchTerm + " " +
temp[i];

                                }
                                return searchTerm;
                            } else {
                                    return "NA";
                            }
                        }
                }
        }
    }
```

2. If the input for the KeywordGenerator class is: https://in.search.yahoo.com /search;_ylt=AqH0NZe1hgPCzVap0PdKk7GuitIF?p=india+live+score&toggle =1&cop=mss&ei=UTF-8&fr=yfp-t-704

3. Then, the output of the KeywordGenerator class is:

   ```
   india live score
   ```

4. We are creating a KeyWordIdentifierBolt class in the com.stormadvance.logprocessing package. This class calls the KeywordGenerator to generate the keyword from the referrer URL. The following is the source code of the KeyWordIdentifierBolt class:

   ```
   /**
    * This class use the KeywordGenerator class to generate the search
   keyword from
    * referrer URL.
    *
    */
   public class KeyWordIdentifierBolt extends BaseRichBolt {

    private static final long serialVersionUID = 1L;
    private KeywordGenerator keywordGenerator = null;
    public OutputCollector collector;

    public KeyWordIdentifierBolt() {
   ```

```
        }

    public void declareOutputFields(OutputFieldsDeclarer declarer) {
            declarer.declare(new Fields("ip", "dateTime", "request",
    "response",
                        "bytesSent", "referrer", "useragent", "country",
    "browser",
                        "os", "keyword"));
    }

    public void prepare(Map stormConf, TopologyContext context,
                OutputCollector collector) {
            this.collector = collector;
            this.keywordGenerator = new KeywordGenerator();

    }

    public void execute(Tuple input) {

            String referrer =
    input.getStringByField("referrer").toString();
            // call the getKeyword(String referrer) method
    KeywordGenerator class to
            // generate the search keyword.
            Object keyword = keywordGenerator.getKeyword(referrer);
            // emits all the field emitted by previous bolt + keyword
            collector.emit(new Values(input.getString(0),
    input.getString(1), input
                        .getString(2), input.getString(3),
    input.getString(4), input
                        .getString(5), input.getString(6),
    input.getString(7), input
                        .getString(8), input.getString(9), keyword));

    }
    }
```

5. The output of the `KeyWordIdentifierBolt` class contains 11 fields. These fields are `ip`, `dateTime`, `request`, `response`, `bytesSent`, `referrer`, `useragent`, `country`, `browser`, `os`, and `keyword`.

Persisting the process data

This section will explain how we can persist the process data into a data store. We are using MySQL as a data store for the log processing use case. I am assuming you have MySQL installed on your centOS machine or you can follow the blog at `http://www.rackspace.co` `m/knowledge_center/article/installing-mysql-server-on-centos`to install the MySQL on the centOS machine. Let's perform the following steps to persist the record into MySQL:

1. Add the following dependency to `pom.xml`:

   ```
   <dependency>
         <groupId>mysql</groupId>
         <artifactId>mysql-connector-java</artifactId>
         <version>5.1.6</version>
   </dependency>
   ```

2. We are creating a `MySQLConnection` class in the `com.stormadvance.logprocessing` package. This class contains `getMySQLConnection(String ip, String database, String user, String password)` method, which returns the MySQL connection. The following is the source code of the `MySQLConnection` class:

   ```
   /**
    *
    * This class return the MySQL connection.
    */
   public class MySQLConnection {

   private static Connection connect = null;

   /**
     * This method return the MySQL connection.
     *
     * @param ip
     *           ip of MySQL server
     * @param database
     *           name of database
     * @param user
     *           name of user
     * @param password
     *           password of given user
     * @return MySQL connection
     */
   ```

```
    public static Connection getMySQLConnection(String ip, String
database, String user, String password) {
        try {
            // this will load the MySQL driver, each DB has its
own driver
            Class.forName("com.mysql.jdbc.Driver");
            // setup the connection with the DB.
            connect = DriverManager
.getConnection("jdbc:mysql://"+ip+"/"+database+"?"
                                                     +
"user="+user+"&password="+password+"");
            return connect;
        } catch (Exception e) {
            throw new RuntimeException("Error occurs while get
mysql connection : ");
        }
    }
}
```

3. Now, we are creating a `MySQLDump` class in the `com.stormadvance.logprocessing` package. This class has a parameterized constructor that is taking MySQL `server ip, database name, user, and password` as arguments. This class calls the `getMySQLConnection(ip,database,user,password)` method of the MySQLConnection class to get the MySQL connection. The `MySQLDump` class contains the `persistRecord(Tuple tuple)` record method, and this method persists the input tuple into MySQL. The following is the source code of the `MySQLDump` class:

```
/**
 * This class contains logic to persist record into MySQL database.
 *
 */
public class MySQLDump {
 /**
  * Name of database you want to connect
  */
 private String database;
 /**
  * Name of MySQL user
  */
 private String user;
 /**
  * IP of MySQL server
  */
 private String ip;
```

```
/**
 * Password of MySQL server
 */
private String password;
public MySQLDump(String ip, String database, String user, String
password) {
        this.ip = ip;
        this.database = database;
        this.user = user;
        this.password = password;
}
/**
 * Get the MySQL connection
 */
private Connection connect =
MySQLConnection.getMySQLConnection(ip,database,user,password);

private PreparedStatement preparedStatement = null;
/**
 * Persist input tuple.
 * @param tuple
 */
public void persistRecord(Tuple tuple) {
        try {

                // preparedStatements can use variables and are more
efficient
                preparedStatement = connect
                                .prepareStatement("insert into  apachelog
values (default, ?, ?, ?,?, ?, ?, ?, ? , ?, ?, ?)");

                preparedStatement.setString(1,
tuple.getStringByField("ip"));
                preparedStatement.setString(2,
tuple.getStringByField("dateTime"));
                preparedStatement.setString(3,
tuple.getStringByField("request"));
                preparedStatement.setString(4,
tuple.getStringByField("response"));
                preparedStatement.setString(5,
tuple.getStringByField("bytesSent"));
                preparedStatement.setString(6,
tuple.getStringByField("referrer"));
                preparedStatement.setString(7,
tuple.getStringByField("useragent"));
                preparedStatement.setString(8,
tuple.getStringByField("country"));
                preparedStatement.setString(9,
```

```
tuple.getStringByField("browser"));
            preparedStatement.setString(10,
tuple.getStringByField("os"));
            preparedStatement.setString(11,
tuple.getStringByField("keyword"));
            // Insert record
            preparedStatement.executeUpdate();

      } catch (Exception e) {
            throw new RuntimeException(
                    "Error occurs while persisting records in
mysql : ");
      } finally {
            // close prepared statement
            if (preparedStatement != null) {
                try {
                    preparedStatement.close();
                } catch (Exception exception) {
                    System.out
                            .println("Error occurs while
closing PreparedStatement : ");
                }
            }
      }

  }
  public void close() {
      try {
      connect.close();
      }catch(Exception exception) {
            System.out.println("Error occurs while clossing the
connection");
      }
  }
}
```

4. Let's create a `PersistenceBolt` class in the
   `com.stormadvance.logprocessing` package. This class implements
   `org.apache.storm.topology.IBasicBolt`. This class calls the
   `persistRecord(Tuple tuple)` method of the `MySQLDump` class to persist the
   records/events into MySQL. The following is the source code of the
   `PersistenceBolt` class:

```
/**
  * This Bolt call the getConnectionn(....) method of MySQLDump
class to persist
  * the record into MySQL database.
```

```
 *
 * @author Admin
 *
 */
public class PersistenceBolt implements IBasicBolt {

 private MySQLDump mySQLDump = null;
 private static final long serialVersionUID = 1L;
 /**
  * Name of database you want to connect
  */
 private String database;
 /**
  * Name of MySQL user
  */
 private String user;
 /**
  * IP of MySQL server
  */
 private String ip;
 /**
  * Password of MySQL server
  */
 private String password;

 public PersistenceBolt(String ip, String database, String user,
             String password) {
      this.ip = ip;
      this.database = database;
      this.user = user;
      this.password = password;
 }

 public void declareOutputFields(OutputFieldsDeclarer declarer) {
 }

 public Map<String, Object> getComponentConfiguration() {
      return null;
 }

 public void prepare(Map stormConf, TopologyContext context) {

      // create the instance of MySQLDump(....) class.
      mySQLDump = new MySQLDump(ip, database, user, password);
 }

 /**
  * This method call the persistRecord(input) method of MySQLDump
```

```
  class to
    * persist record into MySQL.
    */
  public void execute(Tuple input, BasicOutputCollector collector) {
        System.out.println("Input tuple : " + input);
        mySQLDump.persistRecord(input);
  }

  public void cleanup() {
        // Close the connection
        mySQLDump.close();
  }

}
```

In this section, we have covered how we can insert the input tuple into a data store.

Kafka spout and define topology

This section will explain how we can read the Apache log from a Kafka topic. This section also defines the LogProcessingTopology that will chain together all the bolts created in the preceding sections. Let's perform the following steps to consume the data from Kafka and define the topology:

1. Add the following dependency and repository for Kafka in the pom.xml file:

```
<dependency>
        <groupId>org.apache.storm</groupId>
        <artifactId>storm-kafka</artifactId>
        <version>1.0.2</version>
        <exclusions>
                <exclusion>
                        <groupId>org.apache.kafka</groupId>
                        <artifactId>kafka-clients</artifactId>
                </exclusion>
        </exclusions>
</dependency>

<dependency>
        <groupId>org.apache.kafka</groupId>
        <artifactId>kafka_2.10</artifactId>
        <version>0.9.0.1</version>
        <exclusions>
                <exclusion>
                        <groupId>com.sun.jdmk</groupId>
```

```
            <artifactId>jmxtools</artifactId>
        </exclusion>
        <exclusion>
                <groupId>com.sun.jmx</groupId>
                <artifactId>jmxri</artifactId>
        </exclusion>
    </exclusions>
</dependency>
```

2. Add the following `build` plugins in the `pom.xml` file. It will let us execute the `LogProcessingTopology` using Maven:

```
<build>
<plugins>
    <plugin>
            <artifactId>maven-assembly-plugin</artifactId>
            <configuration>
                <descriptorRefs>
                        <descriptorRef>jar-with-
                        dependencies</descriptorRef>
                </descriptorRefs>
                <archive>
                        <manifest>
                                <mainClass></mainClass>
                        </manifest>
                </archive>
            </configuration>
            <executions>
                <execution>
                        <id>make-assembly</id>
                        <phase>package</phase>
                        <goals>
                                <goal>single</goal>
                        </goals>
                </execution>
            </executions>
    </plugin>

    <plugin>
            <groupId>org.codehaus.mojo</groupId>
            <artifactId>exec-maven-plugin</artifactId>
            <version>1.2.1</version>
            <executions>
                <execution>
                        <goals>
                                <goal>exec</goal>
                        </goals>
                </execution>
```

```
                    </executions>
                    <configuration>
                        <executable>java</executable>
    <includeProjectDependencies>true</includeProjectDependencies>
    <includePluginDependencies>false</includePluginDependencies>
                        <classpathScope>compile</classpathScope>
                        <mainClass>${main.class}</mainClass>
                    </configuration>
            </plugin>

            <plugin>
                    <groupId>org.apache.maven.plugins</groupId>
                    <artifactId>maven-compiler-plugin</artifactId>
            </plugin>

        </plugins>
    </build>
```

3. Let's create a `LogProcessingTopology` class in the
   `com.stormadvance.logprocessing` package. This class uses the
   `org.apache.storm.topology.TopologyBuilder` class to define the topology.
   The following is the source code of the `LogProcessingTopology` class with an
   explanation:

```
public class LogProcessingTopology {
 public static void main(String[] args) throws Exception {

        // zookeeper hosts for the Kafka cluster
        BrokerHosts zkHosts = new ZkHosts("ZK:2183");

        // Create the KafkaSpout configuartion
        // Second argument is the topic name
        // Third argument is the zookeepr root for Kafka
        // Fourth argument is consumer group id
        SpoutConfig kafkaConfig = new SpoutConfig(zkHosts,
"apache_log", "",
                    "id2");
        // Specify that the Kafka messages are String
        kafkaConfig.scheme = new SchemeAsMultiScheme(new
StringScheme());

        // We want to consume all the first messages in the topic
everytime
        // we run the topology to help in debugging. In production,
this
        // property should be false
        kafkaConfig.startOffsetTime = kafka.api.OffsetRequest
```

```
                .EarliestTime();

        // Now we create the topology
        TopologyBuilder builder = new TopologyBuilder();

        // set the Kafka spout class
        builder.setSpout("KafkaSpout", new KafkaSpout(kafkaConfig),
2);

        // set the LogSplitter, IpToCountry, Keyword and
PersistenceBolt bolts
        // class.
        builder.setBolt("LogSplitter", new ApacheLogSplitterBolt(),
1)
                    .globalGrouping("KafkaSpout");
        builder.setBolt(
                    "IpToCountry",
                    new UserInformationGetterBolt(
                            args[0]), 1)
                    .globalGrouping("LogSplitter");
        builder.setBolt("Keyword", new KeyWordIdentifierBolt(), 1)
                    .globalGrouping("IpToCountry");
        builder.setBolt("PersistenceBolt",
                    new PersistenceBolt(args[1], args[2], args[3],
args[4]),
                    1).globalGrouping("Keyword");

        if (args.length == 6) {
            // Run the topology on remote cluster.
            Config conf = new Config();
            conf.setNumWorkers(4);
            try {
                    StormSubmitter.submitTopology(args[4], conf,
                            builder.createTopology());
            } catch (AlreadyAliveException alreadyAliveException)
{
                    System.out.println(alreadyAliveException);
            } catch (InvalidTopologyException
invalidTopologyException) {
                    System.out.println(invalidTopologyException);
            }
        } else {
            // create an instance of LocalCluster class for
executing topology
            // in local mode.
            LocalCluster cluster = new LocalCluster();
            Config conf = new Config();
            conf.setDebug(true);
```

```
                        // Submit topology for execution
                        cluster.submitTopology("KafkaToplogy1", conf,
                                builder.createTopology());

                        try {
                            // Wait for sometime before exiting
                            System.out
.println("*********************Waiting to consume from kafka");
                            Thread.sleep(100000);
                            System.out.println("Stopping the sleep thread");

                        } catch (Exception exception) {
                            System.out
                                    .println("******************Thread
interrupted exception : "
                                            + exception);
                        }

                        // kill the KafkaTopology
                        cluster.killTopology("KafkaToplogy1");

                        // shutdown the storm test cluster
                        cluster.shutdown();

                }

        }
}
```

This section covered how we can chain the different types of bolts into a topology. Also, we have covered how we can consume the data from Kafka. In the next section, we will explain how we can deploy the topology.

Deploy topology

This section will explain how we can deploy the LogProcessingTopology. Perform the following steps:

1. Execute the following command on the MySQL console to define the database schema:

```
mysql> create database apachelog;
mysql> use apachelog;
mysql> create table apachelog(
        id INT NOT NULL AUTO_INCREMENT,
```

```
            ip VARCHAR(100) NOT NULL,
            dateTime VARCHAR(200) NOT NULL,
            request VARCHAR(100) NOT NULL,
            response VARCHAR(200) NOT NULL,
            bytesSent VARCHAR(200) NOT NULL,
             referrer VARCHAR(500) NOT NULL,
            useragent VARCHAR(500) NOT NULL,
            country VARCHAR(200) NOT NULL,
            browser VARCHAR(200) NOT NULL,
            os VARCHAR(200) NOT NULL,
            keyword VARCHAR(200) NOT NULL,
            PRIMARY KEY (id)
    );
```

2. I am assuming you have already produced some data on the `apache_log` topic by using Logstash.

3. Go to the project home directory and run the following command to build the project:

```
> mvn clean install -DskipTests
```

4. Execute the following command to start the log processing topology in local mode:

```
> java -cp target/logprocessing-0.0.1-SNAPSHOT-jar-with-
dependencies.jar:$STORM_HOME/storm-core-0.9.0.1.jar:$STORM_HOME/lib/*
com.stormadvance.logprocessing.LogProcessingTopology
path/to/GeoLiteCity.dat localhost apachelog root root
```

5. Now, go to MySQL console and check the rows in the `apachelog` table:

```
mysql> select * from apachelog limit 2
    -> ;
+----+----------------+---------------------------+---------------+--------
--+-----------+---------------------------+-------------------+---------
-------------------------------------------------------------------+---
------------+----------------+-------+---------+
| id | ip             | dateTime                  | request       |
response | bytesSent | referrer                              | useragent
| country        | browser        | os    | keyword |
+----+----------------+---------------------------+---------------+--------
--+-----------+---------------------------+-------------------+---------
-------------------------------------------------------------------+---
------------+----------------+-------+---------+
|  1 | 24.25.135.19   | 1-01-2011:06:20:31 -0500 | GET / HTTP/1.1 | 200
| 864       | http://www.adeveloper.com/resource.html | Mozilla/5.0
(Windows; U; Windows NT 5.1; hu-HU; rv:1.7.12) Gecko/20050919 Firefox/1.0.7
```

```
| United States | Gecko(Firefox) | WinXP | NA      |
|   2 | 180.183.50.208 | 1-01-2011:06:20:31 -0500 | GET / HTTP/1.1 | 200
| 864        | http://www.adeveloper.com/resource.html | Mozilla/5.0
(Windows; U; Windows NT 5.1; hu-HU; rv:1.7.12) Gecko/20050919 Firefox/1.0.7
| Thailand       | Gecko(Firefox) | WinXP | NA       |
+----+---------------+-------------------------+---------------+---------
--+-----------+-------------------------------------------+-------------------
-------------------------------------------------------------------+---
-----------+---------------+-------+---------+
```

In this section, we have covered how we can deploy the log processing topology. The next section will explain how we can generate the statistics from data stored in MySQL.

MySQL queries

This section will explain how we can analyze or query in store data to generate some statistics. We will cover the following:

- Calculating the page hit from each country
- Calculating the count of each browser
- Calculating the count of each operating system

Calculate the page hit from each country

Run the following command on the MySQL console to calculate the page hit from each country:

```
mysql> select country, count(*) from apachelog group by country;
+---------------------------+----------+
| country                   | count(*) |
+---------------------------+----------+
| Asia/Pacific Region       |        9 |
| Belarus                   |       12 |
| Belgium                   |       12 |
| Bosnia and Herzegovina    |       12 |
| Brazil                    |       36 |
| Bulgaria                  |       12 |
| Canada                    |      218 |
| Europe                    |       24 |
| France                    |       44 |
| Germany                   |       48 |
| Greece                    |       12 |
| Hungary                   |       12 |
```

```
| India                     |     144 |
| Indonesia                 |      60 |
| Iran, Islamic Republic of |      12 |
| Italy                     |      24 |
| Japan                     |      12 |
| Malaysia                  |      12 |
| Mexico                    |      36 |
| NA                        |      10 |
| Nepal                     |      24 |
| Netherlands               |     164 |
| Nigeria                   |      24 |
| Puerto Rico               |      72 |
| Russian Federation        |      60 |
| Singapore                 |     165 |
| Spain                     |      48 |
| Sri Lanka                 |      12 |
| Switzerland               |       7 |
| Taiwan                    |      12 |
| Thailand                  |      12 |
| Ukraine                   |      12 |
| United Kingdom            |      48 |
| United States             |    5367 |
| Vietnam                   |      12 |
| Virgin Islands, U.S.      |     129 |
+---------------------------+---------+
36 rows in set (0.08 sec)
```

Calculate the count for each browser

Run the following command on the MySQL console to calculate the count for each browser:

```
mysql> select browser, count(*) from apachelog group by browser;
+----------------+----------+
| browser        | count(*) |
+----------------+----------+
| Gecko(Firefox) |     6929 |
+----------------+----------+
1 row in set (0.00 sec)
```

Calculate the count for each operating system

Run the following command on the MySQL console to calculate the count for each operating system:

```
mysql> select os,count(*) from apachelog group by os;
+-------+----------+
| os    | count(*) |
+-------+----------+
| WinXP |     6929 |
+-------+----------+
1 row in set (0.00 sec)
```

Summary

In this chapter, we introduced you to how we can process the Apache log file, how we can identify the country name from the IP, how we can identify the user operating system and browser by analyzing the log file, and how we can identify the search keyword by analyzing the referrer field.

In the next chapter, we will learn how we can solve machine learning problems through Storm.

12
Twitter Tweet Collection and Machine Learning

In the previous chapter, we covered how we can create a log processing application with Storm and Kafka.

In this chapter, we are covering another important use case of Storm machine learning.

The following are the major topics covered in this chapter:

- Exploring machine learning
- Using Kafka producer to store the tweets in a Kafka cluster
- Using Kafka Spout to read the data from Kafka
- Using Storm Bolt to filter the tweets
- Using Storm Bolt to calculate the sentiments of tweets
- Deployment of topologies

Exploring machine learning

Machine learning is a branch of applied computer science in which we build models of real-world phenomenon based on existing data available for analysis, and then using that model, predicting certain characteristics of data never seen before by the model. Machine learning has become a very important component of real-time applications as decisions need to be made in real time.

Graphically, the process of machine learning can be represented by the following figure:

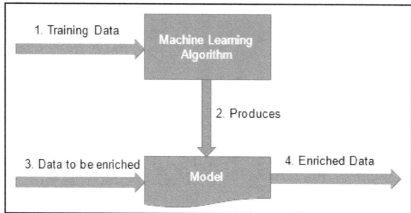

The process of building the model from data is called **training** in machine learning terminology. Training can happen in real time on a stream of data or it can be done on historical data. When the training is done in real time, the model evolves over time with the changed data. This kind of learning is referred to as *online* learning, and when the model is updated every once in a while, by running the training algorithm on a new set of data, it is called *offline* learning.

When we talk about machine learning in the context of Storm, more often than not we are talking about online learning algorithms.

The following are some of the real-world applications of machine learning:

- Online ad optimization
- New article clustering
- Spam detection
- Computer vision
- Sentiment analysis

Twitter sentiment analysis

We will be dividing the sentiments use case into two parts:

- Collecting tweets from Twitter and storing them in Kafka
- Reading the data from Kafka, calculating the sentiments, and storing them in HDFS

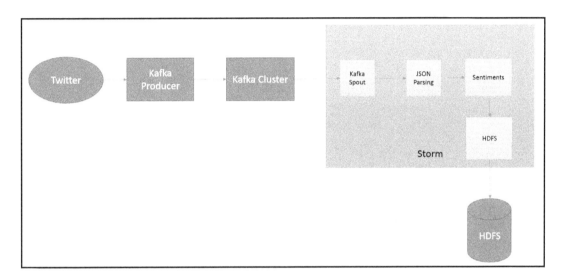

Using Kafka producer to store the tweets in a Kafka cluster

In this section, we are going to cover how we can stream the tweets from Twitter using the twitter streaming API. We are also going to cover how we can store the fetched tweets in Kafka for later processing through Storm.

We are assuming you already have a twitter account, and that the consumer key and access token are generated for your application. You can refer to: `https://bdthemes.com/support/knowledge-base/generate-api-key-consumer-token-access-key-twitter-oauth/` to generate a consumer key and access token. Take the following steps:

1. Create a new maven project with `groupId`, `com.stormadvance` and `artifactId`, `kafka_producer_twitter`.

2. Add the following dependencies to the `pom.xml` file. We are adding the Kafka and Twitter streaming Maven dependencies to `pom.xml` to support the Kafka Producer and the streaming tweets from Twitter:

```
<dependencies>
        <dependency>
                <groupId>org.apache.kafka</groupId>
                <artifactId>kafka_2.10</artifactId>
                <version>0.9.0.1</version>
                <exclusions>
                        <exclusion>
                                <groupId>com.sun.jdmk</groupId>
                                <artifactId>jmxtools</artifactId>
                        </exclusion>
                        <exclusion>
                                <groupId>com.sun.jmx</groupId>
                                <artifactId>jmxri</artifactId>
                        </exclusion>
                </exclusions>
        </dependency>
        <dependency>
                <groupId>org.apache.logging.log4j</groupId>
                <artifactId>log4j-slf4j-impl</artifactId>
                <version>2.0-beta9</version>
        </dependency>
        <dependency>
                <groupId>org.apache.logging.log4j</groupId>
                <artifactId>log4j-1.2-api</artifactId>
                <version>2.0-beta9</version>
        </dependency>

        <!--
https://mvnrepository.com/artifact/org.twitter4j/twitter4j-stream -->
        <dependency>
                <groupId>org.twitter4j</groupId>
                <artifactId>twitter4j-stream</artifactId>
                <version>4.0.6</version>
        </dependency>

</dependencies>
```

3. Now, we need to create a class, `TwitterData`, that contains the code to consume/stream data from Twitter and publish it to the Kafka cluster. We are assuming you already have a running Kafka cluster and topic, `twitterData`, created in the Kafka cluster. Please refer to `Chapter 8`, *Integration of Storm and Kafka*, for information on the installation of the Kafka cluster and the creation of a Kafka topic if they do not exist.

   The class contains an instance of the `twitter4j.conf.ConfigurationBuilder` class; we need to set the access token and consumer keys in configuration, as mentioned in the source code.

4. The `twitter4j.StatusListener` class returns the continuous stream of tweets inside the `onStatus()` method. We are using the Kafka Producer code inside the `onStatus()` method to publish the tweets in Kafka. The following is the source code for the `TwitterData` class:

```
public class TwitterData {

    /** The actual Twitter stream. It's set up to collect raw JSON
data */
    private TwitterStream twitterStream;
    static String consumerKeyStr = "r1wFskT3q";
    static String consumerSecretStr = "fBbmp71HKbqalpizIwwwkBpKC";
    static String accessTokenStr =
"298FPfE16frABXMcRIn7aUSSnNneMEPrUuZ";
    static String accessTokenSecretStr =
"1LMNZZIfrAimpD004QilV1pH3PYTvM";

    public void start() {
            ConfigurationBuilder cb = new ConfigurationBuilder();
            cb.setOAuthConsumerKey(consumerKeyStr);
            cb.setOAuthConsumerSecret(consumerSecretStr);
            cb.setOAuthAccessToken(accessTokenStr);
            cb.setOAuthAccessTokenSecret(accessTokenSecretStr);
            cb.setJSONStoreEnabled(true);
            cb.setIncludeEntitiesEnabled(true);
            // instance of TwitterStreamFactory
            twitterStream = new
TwitterStreamFactory(cb.build()).getInstance();

            final Producer<String, String> producer = new
KafkaProducer<String, String>(
                        getProducerConfig());
            // topicDetails
            // new
```

```
CreateTopic("127.0.0.1:2181").createTopic("twitterData", 2, 1);

        /** Twitter listener **/
        StatusListener listener = new StatusListener() {
                public void onStatus(Status status) {
                        ProducerRecord<String, String> data = new
ProducerRecord<String, String>(
                                        "twitterData",
DataObjectFactory.getRawJSON(status));
                        // send the data to kafka
                        producer.send(data);
                }

                public void onException(Exception arg0) {
                        System.out.println(arg0);
                }

                public void onDeletionNotice(StatusDeletionNotice
arg0) {
                }

                public void onScrubGeo(long arg0, long arg1) {
                }

                public void onStallWarning(StallWarning arg0) {
                }

                public void onTrackLimitationNotice(int arg0) {
                }
        };

        /** Bind the listener **/
        twitterStream.addListener(listener);

        /** GOGOGO **/
        twitterStream.sample();
    }

    private Properties getProducerConfig() {

        Properties props = new Properties();

        // List of kafka borkers. Complete list of brokers is not
required as
        // the producer will auto discover the rest of the
brokers.
        props.put("bootstrap.servers", "localhost:9092");
        props.put("batch.size", 1);
```

```
          // Serializer used for sending data to kafka. Since we are
   sending
          // string,
          // we are using StringSerializer.
          props.put("key.serializer",
   "org.apache.kafka.common.serialization.StringSerializer");
          props.put("value.serializer",
   "org.apache.kafka.common.serialization.StringSerializer");

          props.put("producer.type", "sync");

          return props;

      }

      public static void main(String[] args) throws
   InterruptedException {
          new TwitterData().start();
      }
```

 Use valid Kafka properties before executing the TwitterData class.

After executing the preceding class, the user will have a real-time stream of Twitter tweets in Kafka. In the next section, we are going to cover how we can use Storm to calculate the sentiments of the collected tweets.

Kafka spout, sentiments bolt, and HDFS bolt

In this section, we are going to write/configure a Kafka spout to consume the tweets from the Kafka cluster. We are going to use the open source Storm spout connectors for consuming the data from Kafka:

1. Create a new maven project with the groupID as com.stormadvance and artifactId as Kafka_twitter_topology.
2. Add the following maven dependencies to the pom.xml file:

```
<dependencies>
    <dependency>
        <groupId>org.codehaus.jackson</groupId>
        <artifactId>jackson-mapper-asl</artifactId>
        <version>1.9.13</version>
```

```
        </dependency>

<dependency>
        <groupId>org.apache.hadoop</groupId>
        <artifactId>hadoop-client</artifactId>
        <version>2.2.0</version>
        <exclusions>
                <exclusion>
                        <groupId>org.slf4j</groupId>
                        <artifactId>slf4j-log4j12</artifactId>
                </exclusion>
        </exclusions>
</dependency>
<dependency>
        <groupId>org.apache.hadoop</groupId>
        <artifactId>hadoop-hdfs</artifactId>
        <version>2.2.0</version>
        <exclusions>
                <exclusion>
                        <groupId>org.slf4j</groupId>
                        <artifactId>slf4j-log4j12</artifactId>
                </exclusion>
        </exclusions>
</dependency>
<!-- Dependency for Storm-Kafka spout -->
<dependency>
        <groupId>org.apache.storm</groupId>
        <artifactId>storm-kafka</artifactId>
        <version>1.0.2</version>
        <exclusions>
                <exclusion>
                        <groupId>org.apache.kafka</groupId>
                        <artifactId>kafka-clients</artifactId>
                </exclusion>
        </exclusions>
</dependency>

<dependency>
        <groupId>org.apache.kafka</groupId>
        <artifactId>kafka_2.10</artifactId>
        <version>0.9.0.1</version>
        <exclusions>
                <exclusion>
                        <groupId>com.sun.jdmk</groupId>
                        <artifactId>jmxtools</artifactId>
                </exclusion>
                <exclusion>
                        <groupId>com.sun.jmx</groupId>
```

```
                    <artifactId>jmxri</artifactId>
                </exclusion>
            </exclusions>
        </dependency>

        <dependency>
            <groupId>org.apache.storm</groupId>
            <artifactId>storm-core</artifactId>
            <version>1.0.2</version>
            <scope>provided</scope>
        </dependency>
    </dependencies>
    <repositories>
        <repository>
            <id>clojars.org</id>
            <url>http://clojars.org/repo</url>
        </repository>
    </repositories>
```

3. Create a `StormHDFSTopology` class inside the
   `com.stormadvance.Kafka_twitter_topology.topology` package and add
   the following dependencies to specify that the Kafka spout consumes the data
   from the `twitterData` topic:

```
BrokerHosts zkHosts = new ZkHosts("localhost:2181");

        // Create the KafkaSpout configuartion
        // Second argument is the topic name
        // Third argument is the zookeeper root for Kafka
        // Fourth argument is consumer group id
        SpoutConfig kafkaConfig = new SpoutConfig(zkHosts,
    "twitterData", "",
                    "id7");

        // Specify that the kafka messages are String
        kafkaConfig.scheme = new SchemeAsMultiScheme(new
StringScheme());

        // We want to consume all the first messages in the topic
everytime
        // we run the topology to help in debugging. In production,
this
        // property should be false
        kafkaConfig.startOffsetTime = kafka.api.OffsetRequest
                    .EarliestTime();

        // Now we create the topology
```

```
        TopologyBuilder builder = new TopologyBuilder();

        // set the kafka spout class
        builder.setSpout("KafkaSpout", new KafkaSpout(kafkaConfig),
1);
```

4. Create a `JSONParsingBolt` class inside the package's
   `com.stormadvance.Kafka_twitter_topology.bolt` class to extract the tweet
   text from the JSON twitter tweet that the JSON received from Twitter:

```
public class JSONParsingBolt extends BaseRichBolt implements
Serializable{

    private OutputCollector collector;

    public void prepare(Map stormConf, TopologyContext context,
            OutputCollector collector) {
        this.collector = collector;

    }

    public void execute(Tuple input) {
        try {
                String tweet = input.getString(0);
                Map<String, Object> map = new
ObjectMapper().readValue(tweet, Map.class);
                collector.emit("stream1",new Values(tweet));
                collector.emit("stream2",new
Values(map.get("text")));
                this.collector.ack(input);
        } catch (Exception exception) {
                exception.printStackTrace();
                this.collector.fail(input);
        }
    }

    public void declareOutputFields(OutputFieldsDeclarer declarer) {
        declarer.declareStream("stream1",new Fields("tweet"));
        declarer.declareStream("stream2",new Fields("text"));
    }

}
```

5. Create a `SentimentBolt` class inside the package's
   `com.stormadvance.Kafka_twitter_topology.sentiments` class to create
   the sentiments of each tweet. We are using a dictionary file to find out if the
   words used in tweets are positive or negative and calculate the sentiments of an
   entire tweet. The following is the source code of the class:

```
public final class SentimentBolt extends BaseRichBolt {
    private static final Logger LOGGER = LoggerFactory
                .getLogger(SentimentBolt.class);
    private static final long serialVersionUID =
-5094673458112825122L;
    private OutputCollector collector;
    private String path;
    public SentimentBolt(String path) {
        this.path = path;
    }
    private Map<String, Integer> afinnSentimentMap = new
HashMap<String, Integer>();

    public final void prepare(final Map map,
                final TopologyContext topologyContext,
                final OutputCollector collector) {
        this.collector = collector;
        // Bolt will read the AFINN Sentiment file [which is in
the classpath]
        // and stores the key, value pairs to a Map.
        try {
                BufferedReader br = new BufferedReader(new
FileReader(path));
                String line;
                while ((line = br.readLine()) != null) {
                    String[] tabSplit = line.split("\t");
                    afinnSentimentMap.put(tabSplit[0],
                            Integer.parseInt(tabSplit[1]));
                }
                br.close();

        } catch (final IOException ioException) {
                LOGGER.error(ioException.getMessage(), ioException);
                ioException.printStackTrace();
                System.exit(1);
        }

    }
```

```
    public final void declareOutputFields(
            final OutputFieldsDeclarer outputFieldsDeclarer) {
        outputFieldsDeclarer.declare(new
Fields("tweet","sentiment"));
    }

    public final void execute(final Tuple input) {
        try {
        final String tweet = (String)
input.getValueByField("text");
        final int sentimentCurrentTweet =
getSentimentOfTweet(tweet);
        collector.emit(new Values(tweet,sentimentCurrentTweet));
        this.collector.ack(input);
        }catch(Exception exception) {
            exception.printStackTrace();
            this.collector.fail(input);
        }
    }

    /**
     * Gets the sentiment of the current tweet.
     *
     * @param status
     *              -- Status Object.
     * @return sentiment of the current tweet.
     */
    private final int getSentimentOfTweet(final String text) {
        // Remove all punctuation and new line chars in the tweet.
        final String tweet = text.replaceAll("\\p{Punct}|\\n", "
")
                    .toLowerCase();
        // Splitting the tweet on empty space.
        final Iterable<String> words = Splitter.on('
').trimResults()
                    .omitEmptyStrings().split(tweet);
        int sentimentOfCurrentTweet = 0;
        // Loop thru all the wordsd and find the sentiment of this
tweet.
        for (final String word : words) {
            if (afinnSentimentMap.containsKey(word)) {
                sentimentOfCurrentTweet +=
afinnSentimentMap.get(word);
            }
        }
        LOGGER.debug("Tweet : Sentiment {} ==> {}", tweet,
                sentimentOfCurrentTweet);
        return sentimentOfCurrentTweet;
```

```
        }

    }
```

6. We need to store the sentiments in an HDFS for generating charts or feature analysis. Next, we add the following code inside the `StormHDFSTopology` class to chain the spout and bolts:

```
// use "|" instead of "," for field delimiter
        RecordFormat format = new DelimitedRecordFormat()
                    .withFieldDelimiter(",");

        // sync the filesystem after every 1k tuples
        SyncPolicy syncPolicy = new CountSyncPolicy(1000);

        // rotate files when they reach 5MB
        FileRotationPolicy rotationPolicy = new
FileSizeRotationPolicy(5.0f,
                    Units.MB);

        FileNameFormat fileNameFormatSentiment = new
DefaultFileNameFormat()
        .withPath("/sentiment-tweet/");

        HdfsBolt hdfsBolt2 = new
HdfsBolt().withFsUrl("hdfs://127.0.0.1:8020")
.withFileNameFormat(fileNameFormatSentiment).withRecordFormat(forma
t)
.withRotationPolicy(rotationPolicy).withSyncPolicy(syncPolicy);


        //builder.setBolt("HDFSBolt",
hdfsBolt).shuffleGrouping("KafkaSpout");
        builder.setBolt("json", new
JSONParsingBolt()).shuffleGrouping("KafkaSpout");
        //
        builder.setBolt("sentiment", new
SentimentBolt("/home/centos/Desktop/workspace/storm_twitter/src/mai
n/resources/AFINN-111.txt")).shuffleGrouping("json","stream2");

        //
        builder.setBolt("HDFS2",
hdfsBolt2).shuffleGrouping("sentiment");
```

7. The following is the complete code of the `StormHDFSTopology` class:

```
public class StormHDFSTopology {

    public static void main(String[] args) {
            // zookeeper hosts for the Kafka cluster
            BrokerHosts zkHosts = new ZkHosts("localhost:2181");

            // Create the KafkaSpout configuartion
            // Second argument is the topic name
            // Third argument is the zookeeper root for Kafka
            // Fourth argument is consumer group id
            SpoutConfig kafkaConfig = new SpoutConfig(zkHosts,
"twitterData", "",
                    "id7");

            // Specify that the kafka messages are String
            kafkaConfig.scheme = new SchemeAsMultiScheme(new
StringScheme());

            // We want to consume all the first messages in the topic
everytime
            // we run the topology to help in debugging. In
production, this
            // property should be false
            kafkaConfig.startOffsetTime = kafka.api.OffsetRequest
                    .EarliestTime();

            // Now we create the topology
            TopologyBuilder builder = new TopologyBuilder();

            // set the kafka spout class
            builder.setSpout("KafkaSpout", new
KafkaSpout(kafkaConfig), 1);

            // use "|" instead of "," for field delimiter
            RecordFormat format = new DelimitedRecordFormat()
                    .withFieldDelimiter(",");

            // sync the filesystem after every 1k tuples
            SyncPolicy syncPolicy = new CountSyncPolicy(1000);

            // rotate files when they reach 5MB
            FileRotationPolicy rotationPolicy = new
FileSizeRotationPolicy(5.0f,
                    Units.MB);

            FileNameFormat fileNameFormatSentiment = new
```

```
DefaultFileNameFormat()
        .withPath("/sentiment-tweet/");

        HdfsBolt hdfsBolt2 = new
HdfsBolt().withFsUrl("hdfs://127.0.0.1:8020")
.withFileNameFormat(fileNameFormatSentiment).withRecordFormat(forma
t)
.withRotationPolicy(rotationPolicy).withSyncPolicy(syncPolicy);


        //builder.setBolt("HDFSBolt",
hdfsBolt).shuffleGrouping("KafkaSpout");
        builder.setBolt("json", new
JSONParsingBolt()).shuffleGrouping("KafkaSpout");
        //
        builder.setBolt("sentiment", new
SentimentBolt("/home/centos/Desktop/workspace/storm_twitter/src/mai
n/resources/AFINN-111.txt")).shuffleGrouping("json","stream2");

        //
        builder.setBolt("HDFS2",
hdfsBolt2).shuffleGrouping("sentiment");

        // create an instance of LocalCluster class for executing
topology in
        // local mode.
        LocalCluster cluster = new LocalCluster();
        Config conf = new Config();

        // Submit topology for execution
        cluster.submitTopology("KafkaToplogy", conf,
builder.createTopology());

        try {
            // Wait for some time before exiting
            System.out.println("Waiting to consume from kafka");
            Thread.sleep(6000000);
        } catch (Exception exception) {
            System.out.println("Thread interrupted exception : "
+ exception);
        }

        // kill the KafkaTopology
        cluster.killTopology("KafkaToplogy");

        // shut down the storm test cluster
        cluster.shutdown();
```

```
        }
    }
```

8. Now, we can create the JAR for the entire project and deploy it on a Storm cluster as defined in `Chapter 2`, *Storm Deployment, Topology Development, and Topology Options* in this book.

Summary

In this section, we covered how we can read Twitter tweets using the Twitter streaming API, how we can process the tweets to calculate the tweet text from inputted JSON records, calculate the sentiments of the tweets, and store the final output in HDFS.

With this, we come to the end of this book. Over the course of this book, we have come a long way from taking our first steps with Apache Storm to developing real-world applications with it. Here, we would like to summarize everything that we have learned.

We introduced you to the basic concepts and components of Storm, and covered how we can write and deploy/run the topology in both local and clustered mode. We also walked through the basic commands of Storm, and covered how we can modify the parallelism of the Storm topology at runtime. We also dedicated an entire chapter to monitoring Storm, which is an area often neglected during development, but is a critical part of any production setting. You also learned about Trident, which is an abstraction of the low-level Storm API that can be used to develop more complex topologies and maintain the application state.

No enterprise application can be developed in a single technology, and so our next step was to see how we could integrate Storm with other big data tools and technologies. We saw a specific implementation of Storm with Kafka, Hadoop, HBase, and Redis. Most of the big data applications use Ganglia as a centralized monitoring tool, hence we also covered how we could monitor the Storm cluster through JMX and Ganglia.

You also learned about various patterns used to integrate diverse data sources with Storm. Finally, in both `Chapter 11`, *Apache Log Processing with Storm*, and this chapter, we implemented two case studies in Apache Storm that can serve as a starting point for developing more complex applications.

We hope that reading this book has been a fruitful journey for you, and that you developed a basic understanding of Storm and, in general, the various aspects of developing a real-time stream processing application. Apache Storm is turning into a de-facto standard for stream processing, and we hope that this book will act as a catalyst for you to jumpstart the exciting journey of building a real-time stream processing application.

Index

www.ingramcontent.com/pod-product-compliance
Lightning Source LLC
LaVergne TN
LVHW081337050326
832903LV00024B/1190